The Transition Equation

The Transition Equation

A Proven Strategy for Organizational Change

J. Allan McCarthy

LEXINGTON BOOKS
An Imprint of The Free Press
NEW YORK   LONDON   TORONTO   SYDNEY   TOKYO   SINGAPORE

Library of Congress Cataloging-in-Publication Data

McCarthy, J. Allan.
    The transition equation / by J. Allan McCarthy.
        p.   cm.
    Includes bibliographical references and index.
    ISBN 0-02-920485-2
    1. Organizational change—Mangement.   2. Corporate
reorganizations—Management.
    HD58.8.M333   1995
    658.1'6—dc20   94-36214
                                                                      CIP

Lexington Books
An Imprint of The Free Press
A Division of Simon & Schuster
866 Third Avenue, New York, N. Y. 10022

Printed in the United States of America

printing number

1 2 3 4 5 6 7 8 9 10

Contents

List of Figures

Acknowledgments

The evolution of thought that went into the development of the transition planning process outlined in this book would not have been possible without the help of friends, associates, and clients. It would be impossible to list them all—but you know who you are, and I appreciate the support and encouragement given over the years.

I would like to acknowledge several clients and colleagues who have helped me enhance this work through participation and input or by sharing valuable time and expertise.

Thank you for providing input and suggestions: Randie Bolton, Ed McCabe, Joy McCabe, Dennis Siden, Clay Taft, and Joe Weber.

Thank you to Jennie Schacht for performing a first draft edit with great skill and diligence.

Thank you to Beth Anderson, Senior Editor of Business Books, Lexington Books, Inc., for her effort in shaping the manuscript into a book. The combination of her business acumen and editorial skills made a significant contribution to the final work presented here.

A special thank you for your time critiquing manuscript drafts and offering suggestions: Jim Rossner, Gary Selick, and David Taft.

A heartfelt thanks to my wife Laura, and parents, Jack and Virginia. Laura provided moral support, usually a kick when needed (many were needed), and added great value with her business perspective. Jack and Virginia were constantly encouraging the effort with unconditional support. It was needed.

And finally, to my son Justin, who helped me keep things in perspective. He demonstrated that although writing this book may have been a challenge, there is no greater and worthier challenge than raising a child (two years old at the completion of the manuscript's first draft). I have been sufficiently humbled.

The Transition Equation

Introduction

Managing Organizational Transition

The trouble with our times is that the future is not what it used to be.
—Paul Valery

I remember, several years ago, looking into the bloodshot eyes of an insurance executive. He was in the midst of reorganizing his division and trying to improve the efficiency of the way claims were processed. He said, "You know, I've been at this business for about 25 years. Although I am not close to retirement, I have this feeling that I should move to the country and try my hand at farming or something." He was a tired man—not because he had iron poor blood or wasn't a bright and motivated person. He was tired of trying to cope with seemingly unending changes that incessantly plagued him and his management team.

It seemed like there was no beginning and no end to it. He could vaguely remember how much fun the business used to be. But all at once, it was as though everything had changed. The industry deregulated, competition increased, profit margins shrank—nothing was good enough anymore. Everything needed to be changed. Computer systems were inadequate; employees lacked the necessary skills to perform new assignments; quarterly performance was miserable, triggering an unending wave of reorganization and downsizing. Even the products the company had been founded on and had grown by were mismatched with the market. The company's board of directors, irritated by poor performance, was really applying the pressure now. They began micromanaging the executive group, creating an entirely new set of stressors and frustrations.

The tired executive stood looking out the window, shaking his head. "You know, I think my day has passed in this business. There's just too much going on. I really don't know whether I'm

1

coming or going anymore. It seems like each 10- or 12-hour day I put in, I leave the office with 20 additional hours of work to do. The management group can't get focused. Each week there is a new fire to put out; each month a new initiative to implement. I'll bet we have 50 or 60 projects with number one priorities. It is an impossible situation. Honestly, I don't like coming to work in the morning anymore."

Twelve hundred miles away, in a West Coast bank, a middle manager had a similar conversation with her boss. But her conversation was less positive. Toward the end of the discussion she learned of her termination for poor performance. She was unable to "get the numbers up" in her district fast enough to suit the division manager.

In a neighboring city, two professional analysts had conversed over lunch. It was a typical gripe session ending in management bashing. "Why can't management get their act together and make at least one decision that makes sense? Can't they see that all of the stupid, wasteful projects we spend our time on aren't the problem? Why won't somebody make a commitment to where we are going? Every month it's a new direction. They have reduced staff, doubled our workload, frozen our pay, and then they have the gall to say that everything is getting better. Every time I hear one of them speak, it makes my skin crawl. It's just a bunch of double talk. Those guys are already wealthy; they could care less about us. First chance I get, I'm out of here. Wait until they find out that I'm the only one in the company who knows how to run this order entry system. They certainly will have a mess on their hands when I'm gone."

These are the epitaphs of four American workers, all victims of organizational transition. I have witnessed hundreds of these conversations. They are the voices of American business in transition. And the transitions are numerous and encompassing: increased global competition forcing companies to rethink how they develop and deliver products and services, companies acquiring and merging at a furious rate to gain market share and product base, and aggressive concurrent implementation of initiatives designed to reduce costs, improve quality, and shorten delivery time and to achieve all of this with reduced layers of management and an increased reliance on teamwork.

Over the past 15 years I have worked with 72 Fortune 500 companies and about 150 medium-size organizations in various industries, both for-profit and not-for-profit. These engagements allowed me to closely observe the transitional tactics organizations employ to cope with needed change.

Many management teams in organizations have become initiative junkies. They have no real formula or process by which to address organizational change, so they invest huge amounts of money in popular initiatives: total quality management, high performance work teams, developing sales and service cultures, leadership development, and endless reorganizations and divestments. Rather than let the needs of the organization drive their approach to transition, the transition is driven by the independent directives of various initiatives. This is like remodeling a house in random sequence and without prior thought. Whoever comes to the door first—the painter, the plumber, the carpenter—starts and tries to complete his work without regard for other elements of the overall job. The electrician wiring a room that is not yet framed, with nowhere to hang the wires and light fixtures, gives you a strange look and probably thinks you are a little crazy. It can't be done. In this example, even if you don't know what you are doing, you can't get into too much trouble.

But organizations are not so forgiving. Great amounts of time and money can be invested in activities that are completely out of sequence and for which the workforce is completely unprepared. The initiative, project manager, or consultant is blamed for poor content or execution. Another flavor-of-the-month undertaking comes and goes. Even though little has been accomplished, people may feel gratified. Furious activity was generated, money was spent, the organization had a momentary point of focus and it may even look as if some progress was made. A challenge was presented and more or less met. But has anything really been accomplished, or have the symptoms only been temporarily masked?

What really lit a fire under me to write this book is the recent literature addressing organizational change and transition management. Many works suggest the initiative junkie syndrome described above really does work. Other approaches border on mysticism. They tout a touchy-feely approach to transition, emphatically stating that there is no generic system or approach to transition; each organization must find its own way.

But the simple truth is: Practical and systematic methods for organizational change do exist. They work well. They do not require the organization to change every manager's mindset, every customer's expectation, every employee's attitude or abilities, and everything else about the organization all at the same time. Effective organizational transition is not a hopeless endeavor. Managers having trouble coping with it aren't inept or stupid; it's tough work, far from an exact science. The fact is that good techniques do exist. I will enthusiastically present one such technique in this book that has worked time and again for some of the leading companies in the country.

The Transition Equation presents a practical approach to change. There is a logical sequence of steps organizations must follow to undergo successful transition. Based on many actual case histories, I offer a methodology that facilitates the understanding, planning, communicating, and management of organizational transition. The sequence begins with a well conceived Transition Plan that provides an infrastructure from which to orchestrate all change activities. The organization is then positioned to learn when and how much change it can tolerate and about the sequence of events it must follow. It learns how to reap the benefits of its past initiatives and how to pace the introduction of transitional activities. The entire transitional effort is put in context allowing employees to see how their undertakings will lead to desired future outcomes.

If you are an executive, a middle manager, or simply an individual contributor you have an obligation to yourself to learn the concepts and techniques in this book. Why? Because American business is different than it was 10 years ago. American business is undergoing constant transition.

I have worked with countless organizations that were experiencing long-term confusion, pain, and waste during change. Most of this is unnecessary. It occurs because some well-meaning managers unknowingly institute change strategies out of context, out of sequence, and in conflict with organizational needs. They were working without a context based on their organizational needs.

How many projects and initiatives have you been involved in that have fallen short of expectation or simply don't do what they were designed to do? What is getting in the way? How many times have you said to yourself, "There is just too much going on. I'm not sure what should be done first or second or third." How much time have you spent looking for the answer, or for the consulting guru who says she has all of the answers?

The problem is that the continuous transitions confronting American business are so complex that single initiative solutions and quick fixes won't do the trick. We need to construct a plan that will help us manage during this very complicated and sophisticated transitional period. Our key to success lies in transition planning: creating a clear and tangible roadmap for change. This will be an especially difficult assignment: investing time in detailed planning activity in a "Just Do It" society.

Transition planning is an underdeveloped science. I don't think American business has ever needed to demonstrate advanced abilities in this field before this time. America's businesses have been successful without a high level of planning proficiency because of innovation, resourcefulness, and pioneering spirit. But plan we must. Because most organizations are confronted with such complicated transitional equations, precision planning is the only hope for getting and staying in control. As a manager once put it to me, "You can no longer hold all of the information in your head—it's too complex, too fast moving to plan that way." Transition planning can help provide the infrastructure, an anchor from which to create change. Transition planning can help us understand the sequence of events that must occur for us to move forward. Without it, we are confronted with jumbled priorities, flavor-of-the-month initiatives that come and go with the weather, and confusing, tiring, desensitizing chaos in our work environments. In this book, I share the techniques I have used to help organizations construct and manage an effective transition plan.

How This Book Is Organized

Chapters 1 and 2 are devoted to explaining and exploring the dynamics of organizations in transition and the value for creating a transition plan. This material is based largely on my own observations made in more than 200 organizations to which I provided consulting services. Chapters 3 through 8 are targeted specifically at how to develop a transition plan for your organization.

The last chapter is designed to help you determine whether you need help and what kinds of help you might need as you orchestrate your organization's transition.

Best of luck. You are embarking on one of the most complex challenges life can offer. I participated in a hospital board meeting once where a cardiologist leaned over to me and said, "I'm glad all I have to work with are hearts. They are a lot simpler to fix than organizations." That thought stuck with me. Leading transition is a great challenge—worthy of your effort.

1

The Rationale for Transition Planning

You can only understand something relative to something you already understand.

—Richard Saul Wurman

We are faced with a paradox: Planning in a literal sense is not second nature for most of us. I speak from experience. Writing a book about transition planning was the farthest thought from my mind a few years ago. But I soon learned that the only way to get your arms around all of the details, issues, and initiatives facing today's complex organizations is through effective planning. In this chapter, I explain the rationale for investing resources in transition planning.

The Value of a Transition Plan

I recently worked with a transportation company that was undertaking the massive transition of integrating Total Quality Management (TQM) systems into their operations. They sent 300 management and professional staff to listen to Dr. Deming, the father of TQM, for four days at a cost of $900 per person. This represented a total, eye-opening investment of $270,000! I asked one of the quality managers in the organization what had changed as a result of sending 300 people to this seminar. Did the learning justify the expense?

"Well it certainly increased awareness in the organization. We've been at this TQM thing for about three years now."

"How far is the organization from achieving its TQM objectives?"

"Of course, you know you never achieve perfection in TQM, but you create an environment that tries to get you there, continuously."

"How far away from a TQM environment are you?"

"Probably another five years or so."

"What preconditions or requirements did upper management set to get everybody in the organization working toward TQM?"

"That word, precondition, doesn't fly well in this environment. This company is comprised of cowboys, entrepreneurs, and free spirits. That's how it has grown to a 500-million dollar company over the last 17 years."

"Does some plan exist that literally spells out the steps and the milestones for achieving a TQM environment?"

The reply was rather meek. "We are in an awareness building stage. A more concrete approach and plan will come later."

I agree that quality education is important. I would also suggest that an investment of $270,000 plus 300 of the top managers' and professionals' time off-site for one week deserves more rigorous positioning than awareness building. I state this with conviction because I know of the sense of urgency this company has for performance improvement. Why didn't an organizational plan for TQM exist? As the behaviorist Abraham Maslow said, "When you are holding a hammer, everything looks like a nail."

The management team was proceeding as it always had. When confronted with something new, they send some people to do a preliminary investigation and see if what they learned sticks. In this case, however, the organization was in a frenzy to improve performance. So the "send a few people" scenario became distorted to "send everyone you can get your hands on." This organization suffered from management myopia. That is, they took a very narrow approach to a significant undertaking with substantial resource requirements in dollars and personnel. There was also a high risk associated with unsuccessful implementation, since customers were demanding improved quality standards. Yet, no specific transition plan was in place to coordinate the efforts of the workforce. No milestones drove and measured the organization's attainment of goals. The company spent $270,000 on 300 managers and professionals as an orientation to TQM. No immediate or specific expectations were communicated to the TQM attendees about what the organization expected in return for this sizeable investment. This is a very typical organizational response to new requirements: Throw some money at a new initiative and see what happens. Would you allow someone to remodel your house without a plan, without specific deliverables, without a budget or associated expectations, and without a clear timetable? An architect might argue that remodeling a house is an art form. If he were to be specific up front as far as deliverables, cost, and timeliness it might compromise his creativity and ability to do the work—especially if he has never done this kind of project before. Would you find this acceptable? Then why do we find it acceptable in our business environments?

An organization in transition needs clear direction and focus. It cannot afford to spend time or money on any endeavor that has an uncertain return or is not supported by a plan. Nevertheless, managers tend to engage their organizations in numerous activities that are unclear in purpose. They lack what I call context; a meaningful, relevant, logical, sequential correlation that guides activities being performed. I continually ask contextual questions, "What is the context of this activity?" "How does it fit in with everything else going on?" "What is the logical sequence of activities?" "What is the relevance of this activity to short- and long-term objectives?" I ask these questions knowing that above all else an organization in transition does not want to diffuse its resources, inhibiting its ability to come through the transition successfully.

During transition, the sense of urgency to make things happen can be so high that management tries to do everything at once. They initiate many new activities. But to be successful even during the largest transitions, where organizations must significantly realign their systems, products, procedures, marketing approaches, and technologies, the percent of total change per year will be comparatively small.

If management of companies in transition understand this, they must be keeping it a secret. You would never know it by the kinds of actions they take. Countless projects are started; endless experiments are initiated. So much is going on that it is difficult to know which changes are contributing to the success of the organization and which are wasting time and resources.

In this kind of a noisy environment, critical initiatives wind up in competition for resources with less important ones. As a result, all initiatives are compromised. The message from upper management is unclear. Accountability is low. As a foreman in a processing plant once put it, "No one has to worry too much about doing a good job here because there is always a shift in assignment and direction before you finish." This is a de-energizing and demotivating environment. It is a situation that occurs all too frequently in organizations.

Of all the organizations with which I have had the opportunity to work over the years, I cannot recount one where I did not experience some resistance to the idea of transition planning. Resistance may be based on commitment of personnel and time away from ongoing activities, difficulty getting the right people together, distaste for tasks that are not familiar, difficulty seeing the value of the effort based on past experience where hard work ended up in a drawer, or commitment to the process itself. I could fill a book with reasons people avoid transition planning. It is not hard to imagine why the planning process often gets derailed before it begins. I like to respond to these objections with a favorite story.

A passerby heard a commotion at the end of a long boat dock. He walked out to the end of the dock and was amazed at the sight before him. In a small boat, down in the water, was a group of people furiously bailing water out of an apparently sinking boat. The passerby observed that the boat had a hole and water was gushing in through the bottom. It was a curious sight—frantic bailing while water gushed into the boat through the bottom. It was hard to tell if the bailing was doing any good. The people in the boat were standing in about two feet of water.

Being an unpretentious sort, the passerby sat down to observe the scene further. He ate a bag lunch while watching the boaters bail. After about an hour, he simply couldn't stand it any more. He yelled across to the apparent leader of the bailing party, "Sir, are you aware that your boat has a hole in the bottom?"

The leader replied, "Of course I am aware of that. What a stupid question."

The passerby continued, "How long have you been bailing water?"

"Twenty-four hours a day, for as long as I can remember."

"Aren't you getting tired? It looks like very hard work."

"Yes. But we've devised a three shift operation for bailing. We've even implemented a system for improving our bailing techniques, which has made the job easier and improved our efficiency. You'll note that everyone has been trained on the left arm/right arm rotational bailing technique. There is no wasted motion and it's easy on your back."

The passerby was intrigued. "Why don't you just fix the hole in the bottom of the boat?"

The leader appeared dumbfounded, "Mister, I don't know where you're from, but if you had any smarts at all, you wouldn't be asking ignorant questions like that."

"So I'm ignorant. Tell me. Why don't you fix the hole in the bottom of the boat?"

"For goodness sake! Because if we stop bailing to fix the hole, we'll sink!"

Like the people in the boat, organizations get caught in a similar paradox during transitions. Managers feel an urgency to improve performance. Everyone is focused on improving efficiency, reducing costs and backlogs, and satisfying the customer. The list is endless. Taking time out to conduct an extensive, rigorous planning process is like asking management to stop bailing. If they do, the boat will certainly sink. So how does an organization escape from the water bailing paradox? By becoming convinced that planning will help meet their goals, and ultimately more easily than bailing.

Whether the transition is launching a series of new products to stay competitive or increasing company efficiency to raise stock value, transition represents a critical period for your organization. It is a time when it is not business as usual. In order to protect your livelihood and the longevity of your business, management needs to demonstrate inordinate commitment and participation. Seems obvious. Apparently not, in the case of most organizations I have observed. And what exactly is inordinate commitment and participation? It may involve planning during evenings and weekends. Vacations may be temporarily postponed; travel delayed. The management group should do anything and everything necessary to secure quality informational and planning time together to create a transition plan. Nothing is of higher priority. Nothing. But aren't companies always facing transition? Will this inordinate commitment become the norm? As discussed in Chapter 2, organizations move through cycles where transitional activity will intensify. When this occurs, management must be capable of responding with the same level of intensity.

The root problem is obvious in the boat analogy; there is a hole in the bottom of the boat. Locating the hole in organizations, with their large size and complexity, can be an extremely difficult task. The hole isn't always obvious. Usually the hole consists of many contributing factors which must be dealt with concurrently if they are to be fixed.

Take the example of a manufacturing organization. Over a period of 30 years, this founder-held company grew from a small operation to more than 1 billion dollars in annual sales. Today, the organization faces a compound transition. Its urgency to improve performance is high because profits are down. Where's the hole? Here are some of the factors that contribute to it:

- the founder of the company retired
- the new CEO has a different style of management, less directive in nature
- several back-to-back restructurings have occurred
- defense, the company's primary business, is softening, with a shift to commercial markets
- patent protections on products are expiring allowing competition to enter where it could not before
- core technologies on which all products are based have aged, making them harder to differentiate from the competition
- increased competition in traditionally protected market niches
- an economic downturn
- customers are demanding increases in quantity and quality which exceed the organization's current manufacturing capability, processes, and systems

As you read through this list you will note that some of these factors are outside the organization's control. Increased competition, for example, is just a fact of life. The organization didn't make it happen and it can't make it go away. But about half of this list contains factors that have been instigated, directly or indirectly, by the organization. All of them, in concert, contribute to the instability of the environment, the complexity of the transition and certainly the difficulty in patching the hole.

An organization can easily become overwhelmed by the number of changes that hit it simultaneously. The work environment becomes so turbid that it is difficult to tell why the organization is sinking. As the sense of urgency climbs, management's survival instinct kicks in—try something new, anything. Perhaps restructuring departments, increasing entrepreneurial activities, introducing new training, or developing work teams will help. Does this type of response plug the hole? All may be useful to organizations at certain times under specific circumstances. But undertaking them outside the context of a transition plan is a game of organizational roulette. The workforce cannot be allowed to become diffused, fragmented, or over-committed. Under no circumstance do you want to stall your organization while working through critical transitional periods.

As organizations increase in size and age they develop complex processes and social systems that require greater attention to planning and execution. Often management is simply not aware of or equipped to address this phenomenon. Getting all the right players in one place to sit down and dwell on planning for any reasonable period of time (generally 60 to 100 hours to create a plan) becomes a near impossible task. The result is a piecemeal approach to planning. Each functional area of a business unit—sales, operations, logistics, marketing, administration—develops a list of key objectives and priorities based on the general direction of the group. The result is an unintegrated planning process that invariably generates a long list of competing priorities.

Planning must be a systemic activity, addressing all aspects of an organization and all of its functional areas simultaneously. When a plan is not developed in this way, it doesn't work; most aspects of organizational change require a cross-functional approach and are not responsive to independent interventions. For example, if I want to improve customer service I can provide training to the customer service representatives who handle telephone contact with customers. But chances are that if a customer service problem exists, it is systemic in nature. The actual customer service problem is probably more complex than the way telephone calls are handled. The quality of the manufacturing process will need to be explored, field technical support may need adjustment, warehouse efficiency may be a problem. If we want to fix the root problem, we will need to look at the total organization—its strategies, its structures, and its workforce capabilities. This is difficult to achieve in a fragmented planning effort.

Planning for larger organizations becomes an extraordinary complex task because of the many special interest groups that form within them. In today's flatter, decentralized organizations, authority and decision-making power tends to be more distributed. It is not unusual to find larger organizations with multiple influencial decision-making entities (committees, advisory groups, councils, initiative project teams) located in the middle management and professional employee ranks. These entities can represent powerful special interest groups which must be considered and dealt with during planning.

Another hazard for those not willing to invest necessary planning time and resources is a vague or nebulous planning document. A team of managers from a light manufacturing company spent three days, a total of 24 hours, involved in a planning process. Their leader's conclusion after three days was, "Well, I think we have a pretty good fix on where we are going. I think we need to just go do it now. We have a business to run." The plan, of course, was not finished. Their effort was. When I revisited them two years later, they were back where they had started: 60 number one priorities and not enough time or resources to accomplish them.

A transition plan, like any other planning process, has one paramount value—it establishes context. For example, let's say an organization undertakes 20 different initiatives or major projects (on-time delivery, TQM, delayering the organization), all of which appear important. The initiative junkies get their assignments. Maybe each senior manager in the company champions one or two of these initiatives. A transition plan will provide a context or an explanation for how all of the initiatives will hang together; which should be implemented first, how the initiatives support one another and the contribution they will make to the organization.

The Logic of Transition Planning

Before I introduce you to a transition planning process in the next chapter, I would like to set forth the logic on which any planning process should be based. We plan because we want to accomplish something in the future. We need to figure out the steps it will take to get there. A completed plan will describe a future condition or state which we are trying to achieve and then detail the steps we will take to get there. Anyone should be able to examine a completed plan and learn four things:

1. where the organization is trying to go
2. the specific actions the organization will take to get there
3. the approximate timing for each of the steps and the logical sequence of steps being performed (including other initiatives)
4. the deliverables, and how we will know if the steps (and the transition) were completed successfully

The simplest test of the efficacy of a plan is to look for how closely the daily activities of employees support the specific tasks set forth in the plan. Many organizations have noticeable inconsistencies between the intent of the plan and the way the organization behaves and conducts itself every day.

Another test of the comprehensiveness of a plan is to look at projects, initiatives, and programs in which an organization is engaged. How well aligned are the organization's activities? Do the initiatives support one another? Are they properly sequenced? Are the current programs and initiatives the ones that will drive the organization to its desired levels of performance? These questions must be addressed in an effective transition plan. A technique I use to boil all of the issues down to an understandable level is based on three critical components: strategy, structure, and workforce capability.

Strategy is a specific course of action necessary to help achieve vision or mission statements.

Structure refers to the tangibles, such as systems, processes, standards, brick and mortar, policies, procedures, training programs, and equipment necessary to support the strategy.

Workforce Capability is made up of the skills, knowledge, attitude, commitment, and values necessary to work within a given structure in support of the strategy.

In the following figures are three examples of transition planning malfunctions seen in organizations. In each of the examples the X

FIGURE 1.1
Strategy, Structure, and Workforce Capability, Example #1

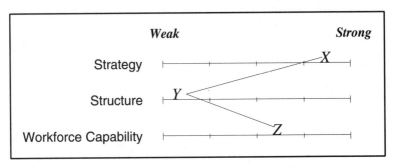

represents a strategy, the Y represents structure, and the Z represents workforce capability. The X, Y, and Z for each example is plotted on a scale from *Weak* (strategy—we haven't described and achieved a goal of this nature; structure—we haven't defined a process, system, or program like this before; workforce capability—we have little skill, knowledge or general experience in this area) to the other end of the range, *Strong*.

In this first example (Figure 1.1), a manufacturing organization decided that it needed to improve the way materials were staged and introduced into its production plant. Management announced the strategy to employees. "We are going to install a new materials tracking system. Everyone will be trained in its use. It will help us all work together and improve manufacturing efficiencies." As indicated by the placement of the X the strategy was well formulated and communicated to the workforce. The placement of the Y indicates that the structure necessary to support the given strategy was not well defined and the organization had little experience in this area. The deficient structure in this case was an outdated computer system used to manage the flow of materials in and out of the plant. As indicated by the Z, workforce capability—the skills, knowledge and general abilities necessary to use the new tracking system—already existed in the workforce. All that was needed was orientation training. In this example, the strategy was formulated and announced, employees received orientation training, but the actual computer-based system was not installed as planned because of software compatibility problems with existing systems. This project was out of sequence. The organization should have been certain of

FIGURE 1.2
Strategy, Structure, and Workforce Capability, Example #2

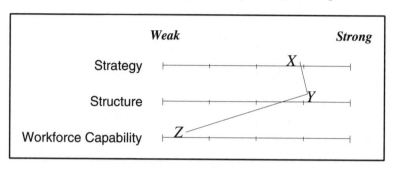

its structural competence before proceeding to train employees. What problems did this create? Employees got excited about the prospects of a new system that would make work more interesting and productive, then became angry because management's promises were not kept. By the time the computer problems were finally resolved, employees needed a refresher orientation training. Poor planning turned what might have been a productive activity into a time-wasting endeavor.

In this second example (Figure 1.2), a large financial institution has undertaken a multimillion dollar investment to upgrade computer systems. The strategy, X, was well defined, essentially taken from a competitor. The structure Y was also well defined. A new mainframe computer system and the accompanying software had already been developed and tested in other companies. As noted by the placement of the Z, strategy and structural requirements far exceeded the workforce's ability to perform within the new environment. The new system was implemented anyway.

The strategy behind this investment was based on what competitors were doing and not directly linked to the needs of the customer base. The skill and knowledge required of employees using the system had not been a major factor in selection and development. The end result was unfortunate. Customer service did not improve as anticipated. Although the new system offered comprehensive information about customer accounts, it dehumanized the customer transaction. Despite increased efficiency, customers perceived reduced sincerity and trust, an important aspect of customer service in the banking business. This resulted in lost accounts. The

FIGURE 1.3
Strategy, Structure, and Workforce Capability, Example #3

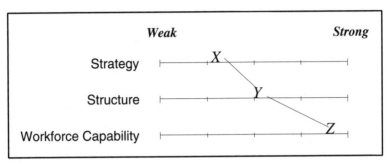

lesson here is that when strategy and structure are engineered outside the context of workforce capability, it can play roulette with your outcomes. Ultimately, this banking organization moved away from trying to maximize efficiency in customer transactions and only used about one-third of the features this new system offered.

In the final example, a large transportation company decided to send all 350 senior and middle managers through Quality Circle training (yes, this was in the 1970s). The training program was quite comprehensive. But as noted in Figure 1.3, a misalignment ultimately undermined the initiative.

The strategy for engaging in Quality Circle training, X, had not been thought through. The structure, Y, of Quality Circles and how they were applied in various environments was well articulated in the training. The workforce, Z, was ready for—even demanding—some new kind of teamwork configuration. Skills, knowledge, and capability to work within this new type of environment abounded.

As the managers came back from the Quality Circle training, they had no overarching goal to shoot for in applying their new knowledge. There was no well-formulated strategy for the successful application of Quality Circles. They didn't know how Quality Circles would help the corporation achieve its goals. As a result, as with all initiatives that lack a clear vision and coordinated plan to drive them, Quality Circles faded into the sunset. As the sun set on this initiative, so too did the organization's enthusiasm for pursuing anything labeled "quality," or for investing the time and money that went with improving it. Employees felt disheartened by another failed flavor-of-the-month initiative.

The importance of alignment and the need for transition planning becomes clear as one examines the repeated failure of initiatives and other undertakings in organizations. Initiatives performed out of sequence or not sufficiently supported can do more damage than good.

Ownership of a Transition Plan

The person who ultimately owns the transition plan is the CEO of the organization (or the highest level manager of the business unit conducting the planning process). A transition plan is not intended to undermine ongoing strategic planning efforts in the corporation, but rather to direct and drive all organizational efforts. The transition plan becomes the context, the blueprint, for change. It is intended to pull all the pieces of the organization's transition activity together where it can be logically sequenced and tested. The plan also governs certain organization-wide activities that must be performed on a united basis to keep the critical mass together while moving through change. Because transition demands cooperation from many parts of the organization, coordination and authority must come from the top. A subordinated transitional plan will yield subordinated results.

2

Focusing Transitional Activity

If you cry 'forward' you must be sure to make clear the direction in which you go. Don't you see that if you fail to do that and simply call out the word to a monk and a revolutionary, they will go in precisely opposite directions?

—George Santayana

Defining Organizational Transition

An organizational transition is everything that occurs after a change or series of changes in an organization. A change occurs and a transition or adjustment period follows until a level of equilibrium or balance is once again reached between the new strategies that drove the change and the structure and workforce capabilities that brought it to fruition. With the birth of a child there is a transitional period in adapting to and raising the child. With a death in the family there is a transitional period in dealing with the void that is left. As in our personal lives, organizations undergo a period of adjustment following change. Some common changes are: deregulation, shift in market conditions, explosive competitor growth, and massive headcount reductions. But given that an organization must remain productive in today's fiercely competitive markets, and that stockholders may not be too understanding of losses, managers may take rigorous, even fanatical action to restore the organization to a state of productivity and profitability. This inevitably results in poor performance during the transitional period.

An organizational transition can be triggered by a change as small as the need to adjust the specifications on how a product is

FIGURE 2.1
Change Impacting Organizations

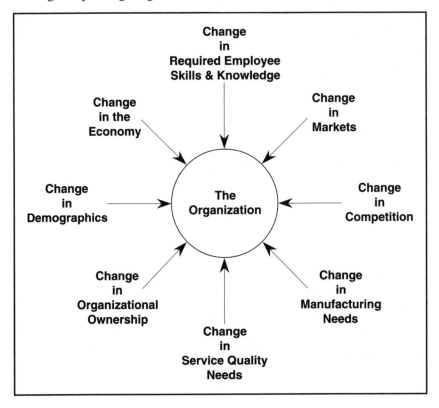

manufactured or by something more significant, such as a change that dramatically alters the market in which the company competes. For example, with the end of the Cold War, defense spending in most nations became de-emphasized. Many companies whose lifeblood had been providing products and services for the military now found themselves caught, needing to redirect the focus of their products and services toward commercial markets.

In today's business environment, change is not only occurring at a highly accelerated pace, but multiple changes are impacting organizations simultaneously. Instead of having to deal with one change event at a time, organizations are dealing with two, three, four, or more change events at the same time. Each change requires some transitional activity on the part of the organization. When multiple changes occur in an organization it takes even more careful engineering and higher levels of skill and knowledge to manage it. In banking, simultaneous change activities have included downsizing, acquisitions, change in product features and benefits, change in customer service techniques, upgrading sales skills, and modifying in-house computer systems to handle new customer service demands. In today's globally competitive market it is not atypical for an organization to experience 15, 20, 30 or more changes at one time. I worked with an electronics company that was experiencing at least 15 simultaneous changes, most of which were significant in nature. They included the retirement of a 25-year founder and CEO of the company; the installation of a new CEO who had a different management style; an increase in competition; cutbacks in the company's primary market which forced a shift into a completely different customer and sales cycle; two reorganizations of the divisional structure of the organization in less than a year; and the organization's attempt to implement Total Quality Management. Each of these changes could trigger a major transition itself. The cumulative effect on the organization, its employees, and customers is dramatic; these changes could threaten the company's very existence.

Examples of transitions that follow change events are:

Economic change: A shift in domestic economics resulting in a need to lower manufacturing costs to keep competitive

Transition: Identify and implement ways to reduce manufacturing costs and begin a migration to off shore manufacturing

Market change: A de-emphasis in military spending shrinks a large, lucrative market which was the livelihood for many companies

Transition: Companies reorient to sell in commercial markets or cease to exist—defense-based sales, marketing, product development and manufacturing tactics shifted to commercial approaches

Competitive change: A new competitor enters the market with substantial financial backing which allows extended price cutting tactics

Transition: Combating this new competitive threat may entail adjusting many aspects of the business, including stockholder dividend expectations and reducing overhead

Leadership change: The CEO is replaced by a leader with a substantially different management style, expectations, and goals
Transition: Realignment of the management team and revision of corporate goals which would ultimately cascade down through the entire organization

A certain amount of change in an organization's strategies, structures, and workforce capabilities on an ongoing basis is good. It keeps the organization dynamic and alive. It keeps employees aware and on their toes. It keeps people adapting to the ever changing conditions of business, markets, and competition. So what is the big deal about transitions? Given the degree of change affecting today's organizations, these transitions are literally tearing organizations apart. A transition can be so complex and encompassing that it paralyzes the organization, disabling it by diffusing its resources. The organization tries to adapt to and address all these changes but winds up trying to take on too many things at once. As a result, the organization becomes horribly inefficient and confused. I am describing a place where employees live in anxiety and pain; where managers scratch their heads, and in an attempt to rectify the situation in the best interests of the company, take actions that only make things worse. Employees say, "What in the hell is management doing? Why don't they get their act together?" Managers say, "The employees just don't care. They are part of the problem. If they are not going to get their rears in gear and help us, as far as I'm concerned, they're gone." One downside to a poorly managed transition, or being in a complex transitional state for too long, it is that the organization becomes a place where people just don't want to be any more. Employees get shell-shocked and fatigued which leads to errors, and this begins to increase rework and critical things simply not getting done. Next customers begin to feel the bad vibrations. They begin to complain about poor service and product quality. A self-fulfilling prophecy is set in motion: People are unhappy that things are bad, so they get worse. In many cases, organizations wind up in a scenario like this because the transition was poorly managed. The transition mismanagement actually complicated the change.

Managers Must Have a Methodology and Skills to Handle Transition

The challenge in managing complex or compound transitions is twofold: The first major problem in managing transitions is that they are simply misread. That is, managers are not schooled in recognizing a transition and determining what to do about it. Many times, market and competitor changes take place around the unaware company as it continues to operate the same way it always has. And when the company finally realizes what is going on, it is often too late. A dramatic example of this is Borland International Inc., a Scotts Valley, California, software company. Philippe Kahn, self proclaimed "barbarian" of the software industry, grew sales from $91 million to $226 million in just two years, 1992 to 1993. He declared "total war" on Microsoft with clever advertising (if you own one of "their" spreadsheets, you can buy the latest version of ours for one-tenth the price), price cutting tactics (leveling profits) and acquiring Ashton-Tate (establishing a dominant position in the database market). The self-induced transition for Borland was immense: competitive war, acquisition and assimilation of a company, and extreme growth. But in June of 1994, Borland International had losses totaling $220 million for three fiscal years and industry analysts are not sure if the company will be able to recover. What happened? The impact of the transition, its size and complexity, was not anticipated. The company was blinded by past success to the signals of impending competitor retaliation while being overwhelmed with the new management challenges of a large-scale acquisition.

Second, management frequently applies overzealous remedies that are disproportionate to the need. The sum total of change required over a period of years may be immense, but the incremental change required month to month may be almost invisible to the average employee. Yet in many, many organizations, the emergency response to transition is analogous to shaking a small aquarium. Everything in the tank becomes unsettled and cloudy. Organizational management teams tend to overreact to transitions and try to do too much too fast without a well-conceived plan. The management team knows something must be done, so they try a bunch of new stuff. If it doesn't work, they try something else. But what generally happens is that this intense, out of sequence activity diffuses resources and sends the performance of the organization plunging further than if nothing were done at all.

A medium-size northeast manufacturer had sagging profits. The new turnaround CEO's remedy was to launch seven major initiatives simultaneously: On-time performance, cost containment, delayering the organization, waste reduction, Statistical Process Control (SPC), Just-in-Time manufacturing, and management training. All of these programs could ultimately benefit the company, if they were implemented properly. However, because there was no plan to prioritize or coordinate the initiatives, many stalled. Manufacturing operators couldn't learn the techniques set forth in the SPC program because their English and math skills were too low. The waste reduction program wasn't effective because it was impossible to accurately measure waste. The current systems were not designed to collect this information and system improvement was not even a project that was queued. One initiative led to the removal of layers of management, supervision, and leads (foremen) but an unforeseen side effect arose: Average plant workers were shouldering responsibility for which they were unprepared. An inordinate amount of time was being shifted away from production duties to logistics management, team development, and administration—all unfamiliar to the operators. Productivity plummeted. The company became a takeover victim and wound up merging with a larger manufacturing company in search of customer base and increased in-house capability.

The same initiatives, sequenced and paced differently, could have yielded a significantly different result. The best method for successfully moving through a complex organizational transition is to equip management with the methodology and knowledge to orchestrate it. After the initial framework is identified, managers can apply their experience and judgment to enhance and adapt the model to serve their individual needs, feeling confident that the basics of the transition are covered. Without a working model or framework for transition, management teams will get bogged down in figuring out how to proceed.

Without a clear transition plan, subcultures frequently develop in the transitioning organization, to work around a disabled executive management team. Think of the terrible waste of time and effort and the inherent inefficiencies of this approach. The best result is that the organization somehow moves through whatever danger the transition was posing, but it does so by further fragmentation and subdivision. An organization in this state is what a competitor might call an easy mark.

During an organization transition, all resources are critical. Plan carefully and stick to the plan. Above all else, don't lose focus and don't experiment too much. If your organization is wallowing, you must quickly and efficiently get it through the transitional window and on to a productive track. There will always be plenty of time for experimentation later on.

Managers Should Strive to Achieve Seven Goals During Transition

In this book, I suggest a proven method for creating and managing a transition plan. Although transitions can range in size and effect from minor alterations of systems and personnel to global changes in manufacturing processes and product emphasis, there are seven goals which consistently surface during transition and which help achieve a smooth transition:

1. align organizational strategy, structure, and workforce capability
2. maintain organizational momentum
3. upgrade employee skills
4. minimize instability by anticipating change
5. identify and follow an efficient transitional sequence
6. communicate frequently and clearly
7. minimize unnecessary disruption

Align Strategy, Structure and Workforce Capability

As an organization develops and grows, so too do its associated strategies, structures, and workforce capabilities. When an organization is productive and efficient there is a balance or alignment between its strategies, structures, and workforce capabilities. A transition can create an imbalance or misalignment of these three

FIGURE 2.2
Align Strategy, Structure, and Workforce Capability

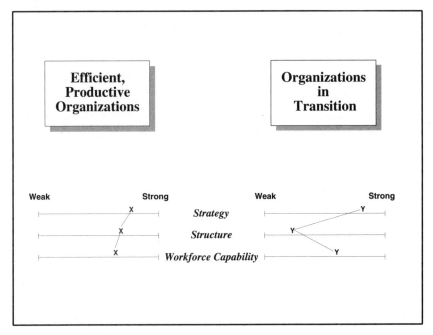

foundation elements and this can have far-reaching effects on all aspects of the organization. For example, in response to shifting marketing demands the organization's management typically will adjust the strategy of the business and thus the objectives of the workforce. Adjusting strategy is not necessarily a simple matter, but of the three organizational elements, it requires the least amount of time and effort. But when you alter the strategy of the organization, chances are that the structure and workforce capability no longer line up or support one another to the desired degree.

Figure 2.2 shows the general alignment of the organization's activities. The efficient organization has its strategy, structure (processes, systems, and controls), and workforce capability (skills and knowledge and employee values) in general alignment. However, the typical organization in transition suffers from the misalignment of these elements. In this case, a specific strategy has detailed the need for a new customer service order entry system. The workforce has been told of its importance and has been trained in its general use, but the system is not yet up and running. As a result, the workforce will have to be reeducated on its use when the new system is ready for installation.

Misalignment can be further aggravated by the naive perspective of management. Many times, the management team has a sense of the direction it wants to take and views the organizational structure and workforce capability as standing in its way. This perspective, coupled with the tendency of management to implement structural "fix it" activities, only heightens the misalignment. Managers frequently believe it will be easier to address the tangible, structural aspects of an organizational transition than those imbedded in the workforce. As a result, they implement many structurally focused initiatives, such as new computer systems, new policies, work team reconfigurations, and new procedures.

This is a major failing in organizational transition strategy. It is illogical to change organizational structure and expect that the workforce will adjust automatically and immediately. This is backwards. By first enabling the workforce—empowering it with a charter and a license to participate in the realignment of the organization—a clear prescription for organizational structure will unfold.

Customers at a large California financial institution had been seeking improved reliability and responsiveness from their bank. At the top of the customers' wish list was assurance that they were dealing with competent, skilled people who would take good care of their money. The bank's primary method for improving customer service was to spend $10 million on the development and installation of a new computer system. Granted, the new computer system was long overdue, but it wouldn't solve the customer service problems. Although the system provided more and faster information to the branch personnel, the system wasn't user friendly. It actually got in the way of providing excellent customer service. The result was a measurable decline in customer assurance levels. In this case, a different computer system configuration or implementation technique might have prevented customer alienation and other undesirable side effects. Yet this organization was not properly positioned to reach that solution because they were driving the transition solely from the structural side.

Management actions worsen organizational transitions when strategies, structural issues, and workforce capability matters are dealt with as though they are discrete entities. This can have a disastrous effect on the organization because it creates further imbalance in an already unstable environment.

Maintain Organizational Momentum

Read the *Wall Street Journal* on any given day and you will see an article about a CEO who was fired while trying to implement strategies that upset the status quo. Each is another victim of organizational momentum.

Momentum is probably the most important and the least recognized factor in the formulation and execution of strategy. To set the stage, I will share an experience that dramatically shaped my own perception of organizations.

At 10 years of age I watched the movie *Moses*, a reenactment of the time of pharaohs and pyramids. One of the tasks of pyramid construction was to quarry large blocks of stone and then haul

FIGURE 2.3
Maintain Organizational Momentum

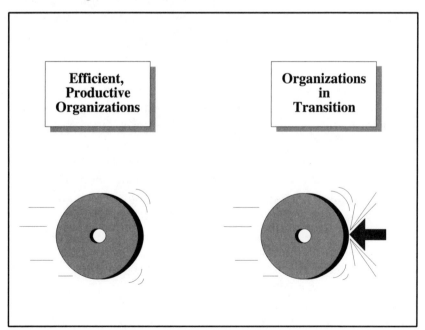

them to the construction site. One scene showed how they actually moved the stone to the site. Probably 1000 men were pulling on a rope attached to a block that was easily the size of a small house. To help the block move across the ground with less friction, workers called runners moved smooth logs continuously to the front of the block. The huge block was moving at a mere snail's pace. One of the workers got his foot caught. No one batted an eye as that 20-ton stone block slowly crushed the life out of him, inch by inch.

As a child, I thought how cruel society must have been back then. Today, as an adult, I realize that this was my first lesson in organizational theory. Because of the size of this organization, 1000 workers pulling on a rope, no one individual or group of individuals could have possibly coordinated stopping the stone quickly enough to save the life of the log runner. Even the head of the construction force did not have the power to stop the block. There were just too many people involved in the activity for it to cease instantaneously. With the increased size of an organization comes increased momentum. Whenever you get a bunch of people all working toward some common goal you will find momentum. That kind of momentum cannot be stopped instantaneously. In this regard, organizations have a sort of mindless nature to them. You can bet that if in the typical large corporation of, let's say 20,000 employees, regardless of what management wants to change, the organization's momentum will always resist efforts to redirect or change it. To deny the existence of momentum is "corporacide" (corporate suicide).

I related this story to an executive of a manufacturing organization several years ago. While I was telling the story he was continually nodding his head. At the end of the story he said, "I've never known what to call it, but let me give you an example of momentum. Years back I was given an assignment to take over a manufacturing division of a company. One of my first actions was to oppose the completion of a product that had been under development for years. It just didn't make sense to me that they take this product to market. In many respects, it was already obsolete. Against the best advice of my direct reports, engineers two or three levels down in the organization, and some peer managers, I killed the project. Guess what? I got fired from that job and moved over here. I'm in the executive penalty box. I think I got run over by organizational momentum."

What does momentum look like in an organization? It resides primarily in structure and workforce capability. Momentum stemming from structure exists in a wide array of forms: policies, procedures, how people are organized to do work, computer systems, and so on. In workforce capability, momentum exists in work routines, skills, knowledge, attitudes, and values. Try to change any one of these items and you will bump up against momentum.

The lesson here is that no one, regardless of position, is immune to momentum's powerful effects. Organizations have an inherent momentum that must be calculated into any transitional endeavor. Whenever you get 5,000 or 10,000 or 100,000 people united and working toward the same objective or resisting something new a momentum exists that simply cannot be stopped overnight. A false sense of security also resides within momentum. If the organization has traditionally done well it can freeze it into not acting when action might be critically necessary.

During an organizational transition, it is typical to see management teams ignore (or simply not acknowledge) the impact of momentum on their decisions. A Total Quality Management initiative or an enhanced computer system, for example, will be placed in front of the wheel of momentum. The result is always the same. Unless momentum is taken into consideration in the way new strategies and programs are employed, the changes are doomed to be run over by it. The echo in the halls of the executive offices goes something like this: "Well, I guess we need to try a different approach to installing Total Quality Management since we haven't succeeded in the last three years on this tack."

A West Coast–based clothing manufacturer was flattened by momentum when it needed to respond to offshore, off-price competition. A thriving $85 million dollar business of seven years was in Chapter Eleven receivership in a matter of eight months because of its inability to overcome limited worker skills, inflexible manufacturing techniques and short sighted union commitments. I look at momentum much like a stock portfolio—unless you have a crystal ball and can predict the future, try to build flexibility into your organization whenever possible.

Momentum does not always work against transition. Momentum based in customer relationships and commitments, service reputation, and market dominance can be highly leveragable. This customer goodwill can buy time for organizations' needing to rethink systems and processes or update products, all lengthy endeavors. A large computer manufacturer provides a good example of the positive aspects of momentum. During the last few years, this company has been slow to market with new microcomputer hardware, because of design problems. Battered by domestic competition with more user friendly computers, it leveraged its size, market dominance, and account relationships to buy time. Today, with a new turnaround CEO, hardware, and software configurations that are becoming more user friendly, the company is offering some surprising performance. Without the positive momentum aspects working for this giant the story could have been very different.

The goal during transition is to determine where momentum resides and how it will work for or against the organization, given the nature of the change.

Upgrade Employee Skills

An organization is simply a group of people united for a common purpose. For example, a construction firm builds houses, an airline transports people, and a bank provides a range of financial services. As an organization grows in size, its employees tend to become more specialized in their duties. From the standpoint of productivity this is a good thing, because specialization allows individuals to become more highly skilled. The downside is that when an organization realigns to new market or product demands, many of those highly specialized workers, once considered assets, suddenly become liabilities; their specialized skills no longer relevant to the new requirements of the business.

Reliance on specialization tends to increase with an organization's size. This explains why larger organizations have more difficulty reacting to market conditions than their smaller counterparts. Organizations that promote flexibility and the ability to adapt quickly (for example, High Performance Work Teams) are less susceptible to transitional obsolescence.

Figure 2.4 shows that over time, organizations tend to nurture and acquire workforce skills which surpass the minimum threshold necessary to perform work. When transitions strike, it is typical to see a significant depreciation in workforce skills. The result is an

FIGURE 2.4
Upgrade Employee Skills

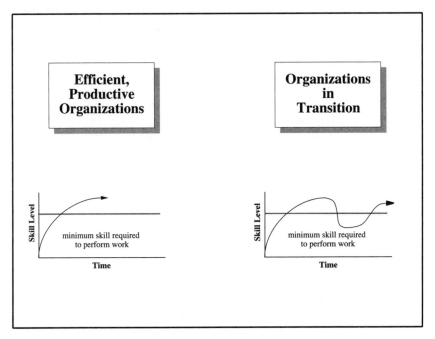

organization functioning below the minimum threshold of skill required to get the product out the door, satisfy the customer, and
make a profit. Given the speed of change in today's markets, it is
not unlikely that a organization can find itself, virtually overnight,
in a position of skill deficit or obsolescence. Of course, overnight in
the life cycle of an organization might be six months to a year or
more. But given the inherent momentum of organizations in general, it is almost certain that a skill deficit position will occur unless
extraordinary strides are taken to keep the organization prepared,
dynamic, and structured in such a way as to proactively meet the
demands of change.

As an example, a key customer requires that its printed circuit
boards, a large volume item, now be made in a two-sided format to
save space. Concurrently, other customers are requesting in-line
quality inspection supported by statistical process control, with
computer reports validating that in-line inspection is being done.
You are now confronted with changing your manufacturing process

and adding new skills and knowledge to the workforce to respond to the requirements of your customers. Workers may need to learn how to operate new machinery, to improve math skills to use the statistical process control system and in general learn to function in this new environment.

One final point about skills. Based on past business needs, it is unreasonable to expect the average manager to be skilled at transition management. Yet most organizations approach transition like any other challenge, expecting managers to roll up their sleeves and dive in. "Transitional Naiveté" describes the lack of critical skills and knowledge in a specific transitional situation. Traditional approaches to strategic planning, organization design, teamwork, and communication required on the part of the management group are not immediately apparent. Many times, management groups do not recognize the need to think and act in new ways. Why is this a problem? Look at the data on business failure. Most never live beyond the ripe old age of 20 years. More important, most middle- to large-size organizations fail during transitional periods. Failure is not necessarily demonstrated by locking up the doors but rather by being forced to sell subsidiaries, downsize, restructure, and possibly give up interests in the company.

Minimize Instability by Anticipating Change

Organizations can be certain that there will always be periods of growth, stability, and instability as they react to change. In Figure 2.5, growth is shown as the two 45° lines drawn left to right. During periods of slow, methodical growth, modest changes to strategy, structure, and workforce capability occur, but these elements remain in general alignment. Even greater stability occurs in organizations that are relatively protected by their environment or by the nature of their product. For example, a dress designer and manufacturer based in New York creates high priced, detailed garments by customer request only. This is an exclusive market niche. As long as the niche remains protected, the business will remain stable.

A high degree of instability occurs when an organization must respond to mergers, acquisitions, buyouts, fierce competition, changing market demands, rapid growth, deregulation, a shift from an owner/founder based company to one governed by general man-

FIGURE 2.5
Minimize Instability by Anticipating Change

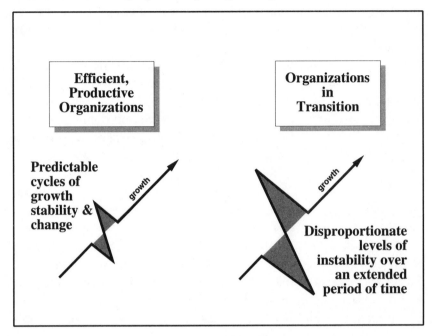

ager, or implementation of a major change initiative such as Total Quality Management. Each of these catalysts profoundly alters the alignment of strategies, structures, and workforce capability in an organization. Periods of instability are probably the most uncomfortable times for most employees whose sense of urgency to innovate and meet goals (whether relevant to the change process or not) is high.

Following instability, the organization moves into a period of adaptation. This is when the ambiguity in the organization's environment will diminish as strategy, structure, and workforce capability begin to realign.

As an organization completes its response to the changes that triggered the original transitional event, it moves back to a period of growth and stability marked by the greatest alignment of strategy, structure, and workforce culture. That is, of course, assuming that the organization makes it through the transition at all. Those organizations that are naively feeling their way along are the ones that usually get buried at this point. If they are not proceeding in a planned manner, it is possible that the cumulative effect of change will diffuse resources (blocking the organization's ability to achieve realignment). The net effect is that the organization becomes stalled in transition.

Some studies suggest that different industries have different change cycles and that there may a correlation between the length of the transitional period and the length of the growth and stability period. Industries that have not gone through a regular cycle of growth and change are equivalent to a highly unstable earthquake fault area that does not have periodic little earthquakes to let off the pressure. Pressure builds and eventually, when it releases, it is of monstrous proportion. In the case of an organization, the source of the pressure is strategies, structures, and workforce capability not incrementally aligned with where the organization should be going.

Banking, for example, was an artificially stable industry for 25 years. I say artificially because it was a regulated industry. In a regulated environment, little occurred to challenge the industry's organizational foundation. With the deregulation of financial services, the trigger event, banking experienced numerous changes that all added up to a compound transition of monumental proportions. The transition began in 1982. In the nineties, with the transition now in full swing, there is no end in sight. Significant changes have included increased competition, downsizing, administratively based culture shifting to sales-based culture, and banks trying to differentiate products and services from those of their competitors when they all look the same.

Organizations that grow and thrive in artificial business environments usually experience the most difficult transitional periods. This is because they are the least experienced with change. Organizations in artificial environments include those that have been regulated, are owner/founder held and governed, grew in exclusive market niches, evolved with little or no direct competition, or have held a dominant market position for any significant period of time. All of these conditions tend to insulate the organization from the normal cycles of growth and change which are important to the organization's vitality and learning.

Identify and Follow an Efficient Transitional Sequence

Sequencing is the fifth of seven organizational transition goals. It is where management has the most opportunity to facilitate smooth organizational transitions.

In Figure 2.6, the various transitional activities are represented by numbers from 1 to 8. The left side shows sequencing in an organization during a period of stability and/or growth. During periods of growth and stability work effort, initiatives, programs, systems changes, and so forth are most likely following an order that is relatively efficient and logical. I say relatively because even in the most stable conditions, some organizations do a poor job of planning and tend to perform work out of sequence. The right side of the figure shows improper sequencing. This may seem like a "no brainer." Why not do the work in the right order? In transitional periods, with many simultaneous changes occurring, it can become extremely difficult to tell what should be changed first, second, or third. Barriers to identifying proper sequence are limitless: an orga-

FIGURE 2.6
Identify and Follow an Efficient Transitional Sequence

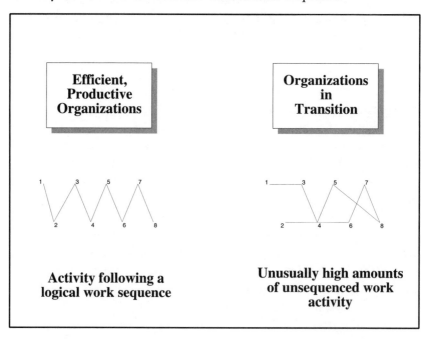

nization's size and complexity including multiple remote global locations, executives promoting their initiative or concerns over the
interests of the company, and a failure to acknowledge that organization-wide sequencing is even an issue. Never should a project,
initiative, or program be allowed to course its way through an organization without its position in the overall transition plan being
deliberately determined.

Communicate Frequently and Clearly

If there is any one signal that tells you an organization is in transition, it is disrupted communication. During normal conditions, organizations have to work at communicating effectively. For example, if the president of a large company decides to visit one of the
field offices, all of the employees at that location put on their best
clothes and are on best behavior. The visit might be friendly, but
the air has a degree of superficiality to it. The president and the

FIGURE 2.7
Communicate Frequently and Clearly

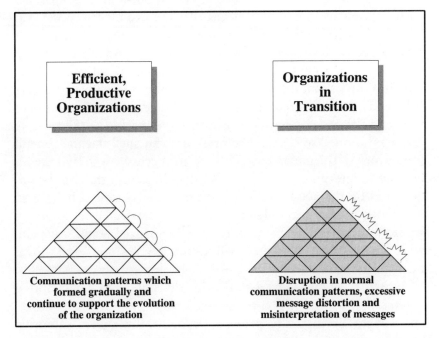

field office employees are not familiar with one another and they have very different perceptions about the organization. The president's view is comprehensive. The field office employee's view is more limited. In this simple scenario there are many reasons communication becomes inhibited:

1. lack of familiarity with one another
2. differential access to information and perspective (upper level jobs tend to be more abstract in nature; lower level jobs tend to be more task based and more finite in nature)
3. differences in job title and level in the organization which trigger certain types of communication-restricting behavior
4. differences in the socioeconomic status of employees in various job classifications
5. variations in educational attainment and the associated communication styles and possible social stigmas related to them, and
6. field office staff are specialized in their functions; the president is not

These and other communication inhibitors limit the range of effective communication, most severely when positions are separated by two levels or more. This means that the president can bet that her most effective range of communication is probably to her direct reports and to those that her direct reports supervise. This is not to say that the president of a company cannot talk to all levels of the organization or that the occasional auditorium speech has no value. It is to say, however, that it is unreasonable to expect the president to the be the primary message carrier to the workforce. She simply is not positioned to do so. The president can spell out the general framework of the message, but it is up to successive levels in the hierarchy to interpret and deliver the news in a form that can be understood by the audience. This is one of the reasons I believe so adamantly in transition planning. If the successive layers of an organization are not tied into the same formalized transition plan, who knows what messages will ultimately be conveyed down through the ranks?

An executive managing a worldwide division of a manufacturing company was faced with a tough dilemma: Find a radically different way to manufacture product or move the entire California based facility to some other part of the country or world with cheaper labor costs. The decision to move the plant would significantly impact the 815 employees in the plant. In an attempt to show concern, to be open and honest and involve his employees in this difficult long range decision, he decided to share what he knew with all of the employees. He assembled the division in an auditorium. He told them that in six months to a year he would have enough data to make a decision: keep the plant here or move it. In an analytical, matter-of-fact tone, he explained the economic issues, the current strategic analysis underway and at what point they could expect a decision. At the conclusion of his presentation, he asked for questions from the hushed audience. A machinist raised his hand and asked if he could speak to the executive in private after the meeting. The executive said that no question was too private, go ahead and ask. The machinist said he just wanted an opportunity to beat his face in. The executive deserves credit for being honest, but undermined the effectiveness of his presentation by not showing more concern, asking for their input, or explaining how the company would deal with layoffs if they became necessary. As a result, the employees went into emotional overload. In this same division, sabotage, work slow-down, and high absenteeism followed the presentation. This eliminated the slim possibility of keeping the manufacturing facility local.

Transitions create all kinds of havoc with normal communication channels. As the leaders of an organization try to come to grips with what needs to be done, the workforce watches and waits. Effective communication dwindles as top management sends out either no information or mixed signals while trying to figure out what to do next. The workforce becomes overloaded with conceptual messages it cannot understand. As messages are handed down the hierarchy, those that are abstract and unclear get distorted and ultimately misunderstood or simply lost.

Environmental instability, which triggers confusion, fear, and anger in the workforce produces a lot of "noise." When employees are upset, it is difficult to get their attention—to get a coherent message delivered. In this environment it becomes difficult to know if what you are hearing is real. Employees second guess everything they are told; they begin taking even routine communications with a grain of salt. When employees are overloaded with information, they become selective listeners. Although you might have a room of 20 people listening to a manager discuss a new and important activity, when those 20 people leave the room, they leave with 20 different interpretations of the same presentation. Information overload can potentially clog up the normal communication channels and render them dysfunctional.

Minimize Unnecessary Disruption

When we talk about change and how it affects employees, we are obliged to discuss behavior. Behavior, a specific action we take, usually is associated with a routine. A behavior, for example, is wiping a machine with a cleaning compound. The routine is all the behaviors necessary to clean the machine and ready it for production. During transition, routines that made a lot of sense when they were originally formed and learned can become outdated and no longer make sense. But it is not apparent to us because we tend to perform them automatically. We purposely conditioned ourselves that way to deal efficiently with the complexities of our environment. It is very difficult to step outside this environment, to evaluate our actions relative to their value and purpose as part of the total organization. This is especially true because most of us have an extremely limited exposure to all aspects of the organization. We are beyond questioning why we do it this way or that. This is also why the Total Quality Management movement professes that the only way we can create an effective quality improvement process is through individual self-examination and adjustment of the processes on which we base our behavior. This stops the autopilot behavior patterns and forces us to rethink them.

There is a predictable series of reactions that people go through in response to routine disruption. This reaction pattern can be seen in organizations undergoing large-scale change. With work routines disrupted, employees become confused. "Things are not the way they should be!" "I'm not going to do anything that might put me out on a limb. I'm simply going to lie low; wait and see." The work environment becomes foreign and uncomfortable. Next workers become fearful. "Can I cope with the new assignments?" "Am I capable enough to handle the job?" "Will I get fired if I don't adapt quickly enough?" And finally, they are angry. "Somebody at the top doesn't know what it is like down here." "I think this is just a plot to get rid of some of the longer-term, better paid employees to cut company costs." "We'll eventually get back to how we used to do things. Everything goes full circle." "I don't think I am in danger of losing my job, but first chance I get, I'm out of here. Nobody plays mind games on me like this. Nobody. Screw 'em."

We are presented with a paradox during change. On one hand we probably want the workforce to reexamine how it is doing its routine work and incorporate anything that can contribute to transition. Conversely, we don't want to get too carried away and change routines that don't need to be altered. Nor do we want to get too much going on at once so that we become overwhelmed, slowing down progress. Major transitions can disrupt worker routines on such a massive scale that the workforce can be nearly paralyzed. I call this an anxiety cycle—too many routines are changed simultaneously so that employees begin experiencing first confusion, then fear, and finally anger.

The question every manager must ask is, "What impact does it have on the organization when a large percentage of my employees are experiencing an anxiety cycle?" The answer is, "significant impact." Anxiety can negatively influence all transitional activities. But there is also a positive side to anxiety cycles: People feel so uncomfortable once they enter one that their urgency to re-establish routines and stabilize their lives is high. This can be a powerful motivator when redirecting the activities of employees as long as the anxiety cycle is controlled and short-lived and a clear transitional roadmap to the future accompanies the routine disruption. Sustained anxiety cycles ultimately reduce performance and destroy motivation.

Examples of events that disrupt routines and create anxiety cycles are all around us. A friend going through a divorce might be emotionally devastated. Another acquaintance may be experiencing an equal amount of stress as a prelude to marriage. Marriage, however, usually offers positive routine replacement; divorce can leave a void filled with long-term emotional land mines. Divorce may also be the catalyst to break unhealthy routines; this can be very positive.

From an organizational transition perspective, anticipating the impact the transition will have on work routines can provide powerful information and guidance. We want employees to perform in a new way, but we don't want to traumatize them in the process. Otherwise we might wind up with an organization of thousands of people all at some stage in the anxiety cycle. Imagine the impact on productivity if all 20,000 employees in the company experienced either a death in the family or a divorce simultaneously. And one wonders why so many organizations sputter during a transitional period, when everybody's routines are radically altered.

We must also consider that, although work is a major portion of our lives, most employees are in fact dealing with their own personal transitions outside the work environment. People have a limit to the amount of stress and anxiety they can handle at one time. If, hypothetically, each person has 100 units of anxiety to spend per year, and any amount over 100 units throws the person into an anxiety cycle, then what portion of this 100 units is available to spend on the job? The answer is probably not much more than half. But many organizations, given the nature of their transitions and the tactics, or more realistically the lack of tactics, used to move through them, unknowingly demand 200 units of anxiety from employees, exceeding their fair share by 4 times. The result is employees at all organizational levels are fighting to stay on an even keel. Their focus leaves their work. They begin acting out of pattern. Productivity dives, just the opposite of what management was trying to achieve. Work effort becomes diffused. Accomplishing even some of the simplest tasks becomes somehow all consuming.

The effect of organizational transition on the employees is observable. It is not difficult to immediately pick out people who are handling transitional activity well, or those who have slipped into the anxiety cycle. An organization's state of transition can be read by simply listening to what a sampling of employees are saying, without even looking at the strategic and structural components.

Are any of these statements heard in your organization?

- "It's just no fun any more."
- "It's impossible to provide quality service when we're this short-handed."
- "The pace is ridiculous. Each month we have higher goals with fewer employees."
- "I've been with this organization for 20 years and now they're after my rear."

- "I hope somebody knows what's going on."
- "It's obvious that the company doesn't care about the customer any more. They just want their money."
- "There used to be a future in this job. Now there is no career path and I'll be lucky to keep my job."
- "Every day when I come to work they change the game again. Most people in my department are working at about 20 percent capacity. It's no wonder we can't get anything done."
- "I really don't believe that senior management has a handle on things. I'm not in the minority in this view. I really wonder, if it appears so obvious to me, why can't they (top management) see what's going on?"
- "I've learned that my job is going away. I'm going to make them pay in ways they can't imagine."
- "I'm burned out. I just can't stay focused on work. The rumor mill is rampant and every time I hear something, I get upset and can't get my projects done."

These statements are just a sampling of employee statements expressing their confusion, fear, and anger. They are based on very real and genuine feelings. They are expressions that indicate discord and misunderstanding with the organization's transition. And they can provide significant insight into how well a transition is being managed.

Knowledge about workforce routines gives a manager a distinct advantage during transitional periods. The trick becomes translating this knowledge into a practical, usable format. Too many approaches to transition turn out to be fragmented, analytical overkill or to be busy-work activity—nothing really productive. The end product is, of course, of no benefit to anyone, other than possibly making some manager somewhere feel better because something is being done. Many transitional activities have less to do with helping the organization through its transition and more to do with generating activity for activity's sake. I read an article once that described an interesting approach to management development and motivation. It said that when you have a large cage of canaries, you need to bang on top of the cage periodically to keep them all flying. The theory was that the same held true for managers. The CEO needs to structure activities to make sure he keeps the management group flying. The supposition is that a lot of activity translates to a lot of productive activity. But this analogy describes what is wrong with many transition activities. Activities are done more for the sake of satisfying the need to do something, rather than within the context of a meaningful transition plan.

Awareness and deliberate consideration of these seven overarching goals will contribute to a smooth transition. In the next chapter we explore how to create a transition plan.

3

How to Create a Transition Plan

The complexity of contemporary states seems to break down any single mind that tries to master it.

—Will and Ariel Durant

In this chapter we will take a close look at how to create a transition plan. Before your eyes glaze over and roll back in your head, let me restate that transition planning doesn't have to be a boring, arduous task. The transition planning process can be exciting if it provides a platform for organizational learning and identifies a clear route to the future with specific steps to get there. Planning can be reassuring when it results in focus and even protection; protection against too many priorities, too many initiatives, and the confusion that tends to permeate transitioning environments.

Assembling the Right Team

In order to construct a transition plan that serves your needs, you first must deal with a tough issue: Do you have the talent in-house to do it? This is not a sales pitch for hiring external consultants. But you must have the right mix of knowledge and experience to build a plan that will get you where you want to go.

In order to climb to the executive ranks most managers develop an air of impenetrability about them. Executives are not in the habit of saying, "I don't know how to do that." Show me one that is, and I'll show you an unemployed executive. It is safe to assume that when you assemble the senior management team, the perception of what talent you have and don't have will be distorted for this reason. That makes assembling the right team even more critical. Chances are, you will overestimate the abilities of your group.

Here are several simple tests you can use to see if your planning team has the right mix of knowledge and experience:

- 30 percent of members should have direct experience creating and managing an organizational transition.
- 30 percent of members should have experience in at least five or more different organizations.
- 30 percent of members should have formal education in management and planning.
- 30 percent of the members should have long-term, comprehensive experience with the company for which the plan is being crafted.
- The organization's strategic planner should be included and should have direct experience in managing organizational transition with at least 20 different businesses.
- There must be a consensus that the organization is undergoing transition.
- The leader of the group should have the authority and ability to make decisions for the group, when necessary.

If your team doesn't meet these standards, you should take this as a red flag. Any prudent organization should, as a matter of course, look for a balance of participants in the planning process that can contribute competitor and customer experience, business intuition and vision, process thinking, and general knowledge about the company's business. Additions to this core group should be considered, including planners and other key staff or line employees that are unusually predisposed to the planning work that lies ahead. There are such people in the typical organization.

A universal sense of urgency and commitment must prevail in the attitudes and actions of the transition planning team. Planning processes become bogged down when members of the team do not make themselves available. A transition is a time when calendars must be cleared and vacations and other commitments must be rearranged to accommodate the needs of the planning process. If your team is unwilling to do this, they are not taking the task at hand seriously enough.

Another way to add depth to your planning team is to form an advisory group. An advisory group would serve as mentors to the transition planning team. An external advisory group (not employees of the company) could consist of several external consultants and loaned executives not unlike the arrangements used to solicit other industry leaders as members of a board of directors. The individuals who generally contribute the most are those who have had hands-on, direct experience in organizational transition. This means that they have consulted with or directly managed an organization involved in a significant change event. It is not necessary that their transition experience be directly related—the quantity and variety of experience is what amplifies skills in this area. Be wary of theorists who appear esoteric or difficult to understand. They may have great ideas, but chances are that if you can't easily understand what they profess, their great ideas are skewed more toward theory than practical application. You do not want to be someone else's testing ground during a transition.

An internal advisory group is a foreign concept to many executives. The reason: If the transition planning team consists of the highest executives in the company, why form an advisory group of underlings—employees of less status and experience? The simple answer is that the highest executives in the company may have the best strategic information available, but limited current knowledge on the operational side. An internal advisory group would tend to offer grounding in practicalities that might be difficult to surface elsewhere.

The role of an advisory group—external, internal, or a combination of both—is to offer additional perspective and nonpartisan input. It is best that the advisory group function independently and be attached only to the CEO.

I would not recommend advisory group members as permanent participants with the transition planning team. This type of collaboration is more complex and may have a number of pros and cons associated with it. For example, an external advisory group member may have a vested interest in the success of the business, but generally external advisors don't have day-to-day knowledge of business operations. Transition planning reaches a level of operational detail that is too specific for this type of advisory group.

When you have assembled the right team, you will have a genuine balance of internal and external perspective and experience.

You will have members sitting at the table that have been through a transition before. You will have members sitting at the table that know the business inside and out. You will have neutralized political factions and the group's tendency to polarize. You will have proper depth of perspective. You will have an ultimate decision-maker who will keep the group focused and moving forward. You will have a commitment by all involved to invest the necessary time to see the transition planning process to its completion. Now it is simply a matter of following a logical, methodical, and systematic transition planning process that will get you the results you seek.

Transition represents a critical period for your organization, whether the transition is introducing a new product, restructuring the organization, or learning to compete in a changing market environment. Choose your help carefully. Transitions don't start or end in a day. Even though the urgency may be high to get a plan in place—which means get help—invest time to methodically, thoroughly contemplate your options.

Five Key Steps of a Transition Plan

The general framework for the transition plan that follows is based on both the mechanical and practical aspects of organizational change. Many of the Transition Plan's key elements appear obvious; logical things to do. In fact, many managers believe they already are doing or have done them. But they have not completed a successful transition—perhaps because the elements were performed out of sequence or because they were not performed thoroughly enough to derive the intended benefit. The five key steps of a transition plan are:

- describe the future state
- identify transition preconditions
- evaluate present transitional abilities
- develop an incremental master plan
- communicate transitional activity

Although each planning team will follow a unique process, I suggest that you do not alter the infrastructure proposed here. It will prevent you from taking shortcuts that could possibly subordinate your planning process. Let's look at each of these five steps in greater depth and discuss why each should be included in your transition plan. Chapters 4 through 8 are devoted to the actual construction of a transition plan based on these steps.

Step One: Describe the Future State

The purpose in identifying a future state is to describe what the organization is going to be like when the transition is complete. It is not enough to articulate a direction for the company. The future must be described in specific terms. It may be true that the destiny of an organization is always evolving and changing, but this does not mean this step is unnecessary in creating a plan. The desired product at the completion of this stage is a vision and/or mission document (the document you produce here depends on the level and focus of the planning group) that can be translated into specific actions the organization must take to achieve their vision. The translation takes place in steps three and four of the planning process.

Remember, planning is dynamic. It should be performed regularly. As the goals and objectives of the organization change, the plan is adjusted to align the organization's strategy, structure, and workforce capability. Organizations that create very general vision and mission statements have great difficulty deploying them. Generalized documents allow too much room for interpretation and may not be translatable. Where business unit managers really earn their money—whether the CEO, division manager, or unit manager—is in articulating in specific terms the vision and mission of the company's future.

FIGURE 3.1
Elements of a Transition Plan—Step One

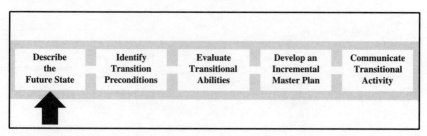

Chapter 4 explains how to describe the future state in a way that will truly be useful to your organization.

Step Two: Identify Transition Preconditions

Before an organization develops a plan to move forward, it must identify the roadblocks in its path. These obstacles can be internally constructed, such as inadequate employee skills or pervasive bureaucracy, or they can be external, such as government regulation or a dwindling customer base. Acknowledging preconditions in the planning process makes it less likely that they will derail the implementation.

Generally speaking, preconditions are not difficult to identify. They can be, however, hard to address because they tend to be intertwined in organizations, making them politically difficult to untangle. This is where the CEO or the head of the business unit involved in planning earns his keep. The chief executive officer must, at times, step across all boundaries and mandate compliance for the betterment of the organization. For example, to improve coordination among business units the CEO might require each to create and share their plans in a similar format and on a similar schedule.

When the obstacles to transition are deeply imbedded in the infrastructure of the organization, the organization will energetically resist any changes, and organizational momentum will play a major role. I recently worked with a middle-size European shipping company. Because of company and country union systems, any changes to pay, position, work procedures, and resource allocation were painfully slow. This did not preclude changes. It did pose a series of obstacles as to how, when, and where the changes could be made.

FIGURE 3.2
Elements of a Transition Plan—Step Two

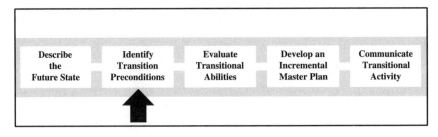

| Describe the Future State | Identify Transition Preconditions | Evaluate Transitional Abilities | Develop an Incremental Master Plan | Communicate Transitional Activity |

Identifying transition preconditions and including them in the transition plan reduces organizational fragmentation by providing reality check points. It helps prevent employees from simply using up resources on activities that may be predestined to failure. Identification of preconditions also ensures that existing management commitments and organizational limitations are acknowledged and incorporated in the plan—they are adequately taken into account and addressed in the transition plan.

Chapter 5 presents a detailed technique for identifying transition preconditions.

Step Three: Evaluate Transitional Abilities

Once the future direction of the company is determined and transition preconditions are identified, it is important to fully comprehend what actions will be required to achieve this desired state.

Traditionally, vision and mission statements are formulated and described in terms of overarching objectives: the organization's goals over the next several years. Where these documents fall short is that the planning team has not described the strategies, structures, and workforce capabilities necessary to support the objectives. A translation needs to occur that accomplishes two things: identifies what we are required to do and how capable we are of doing it.

In this step, planning equations are used to identify the strategy, structure, and workforce capability necessary to achieve the future state—how the company's vision or business unit's mission will actually translate into reality. It will help identify and bring into focus

FIGURE 3.3
Elements of a Transition Plan—Step Three

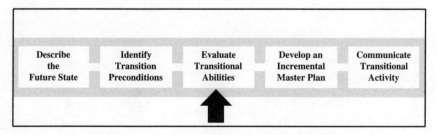

what the planning team really had in mind. Some objectives implicit in the future state will be adjusted because, although they sounded great, when viewed with the entire equation they turn out to be completely inappropriate for the organization.

Step Four: Develop an Incremental Master Plan

Organizations seldom have the luxury of working on one thing at a time. The real issue is finding the time and resources to undertake 20 initiatives or projects simultaneously. An incremental master plan establishes a sequence for all of the organization's initiatives. It should contain all of the projects, goals, and change initiatives included in the organization's transition, including work in progress. The master plan will provide a context for change, a logical sequence of activities that closely match the organization's ability to perform them, and will prevent the various business units from straying too far on tangents that could diffuse resources and deter the organization from its ultimate objective. A master plan will help prevent the interruptions and duplication that occur when one or more initiatives are performed out of sequence. It also prevents a driven executive who, oblivious to the needs of the total organization, interferes with other activities by promoting an initiative which may be out of sequence.

Sequencing, making sure that activities occur in the most logical order, is not the same as prioritization. Prioritizing projects should be a matter of determining their overall importance to the organization, not the order in which they should occur. With few exceptions, if you carefully examine a list of prioritized activities you will

FIGURE 3.4
Elements of a Transition Plan—Step Four

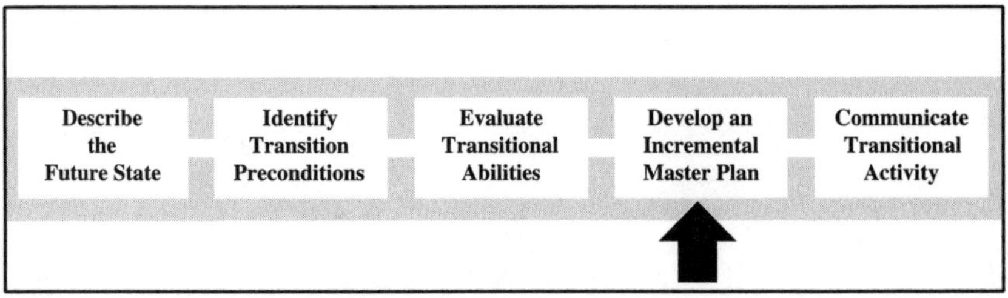

| Describe the Future State | Identify Transition Preconditions | Evaluate Transitional Abilities | Develop an Incremental Master Plan | Communicate Transitional Activity |

find that certain low priority activities actually need to occur before many high-priority activities can be performed. Performing activities in priority order but out of sequence results in duplication of effort, missed opportunities, and generally slower, more difficult work activity. There always seems to be something getting in the way of progress.

In Chapter 7 we will review techniques for developing an incremental master plan.

Step Five: Communicate Transitional Activity

No one argues against communicating; it is a given that communication is critical in organizations. Yet most organizations, especially those in transition, would admit that they don't have effective communication systems. Employees simply are not listening or are too anxious and distracted to understand the messages sent down through traditional channels. In transitional environments, management does a lot of thinking on its feet. The result is that many directives and other messages sent through the organization are not fully thought through, are too vague, or simply are incomplete. This further compounds the misunderstanding and confusion inherent in the transitioning environment.

Communication should precede any transitional effort. So the first action is always to tell everyone and anyone that you are engaging in a five-stage transitional planning effort and you will update them periodically.

Communication, and communication planning, are pivotal. Once the preceding four transition planning steps are adequately

FIGURE 3.5
Elements of a Transition Plan—Step Five

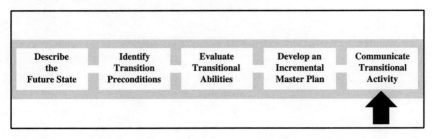

| Describe the Future State | Identify Transition Preconditions | Evaluate Transitional Abilities | Develop an Incremental Master Plan | Communicate Transitional Activity |

addressed, everything learned must be disseminated throughout the organization. The messages must be clear, be repeated enough to get through, be completely consistent with all other messages, and be sent through a variety of channels to ensure they reach the entire audience.

Perception management, a critical part of communicating during change, may be the single most important activity in the transition planning process. Each of the stakeholders—customers, employees, suppliers, partners, and others that hold an interest in your organization—have some influence over your job longevity. Your stakeholders must believe that you are in control and achieving the desired results. If they don't perceive this, you will never get a chance to fully implement your transition plan. Unless you invest in understanding your stakeholders' perceptions about your transition efforts, all may be for naught. This topic is addressed more extensively in Chapter 8.

These five steps are the proven framework for effective transition. Whether your organization is changing because of radically different market trends or is introducing a whole new organizational structure, the transition will go faster and smoother if these five steps are followed. It may appear to be an overwhelming, time consuming endeavor. It doesn't have to be, and you don't have to get everything perfect the first time. Organizations continuously change; a plan must be dynamic as well. But a commitment must be made to embrace transition planning completely. I remember a saying, "Don't be afraid to take a big step if one is indicated. You can't cross a chasm in two small jumps." Likewise, transition planning can't be accomplished in little steps. Plan well and take the challenge.

4

Describe the Future State

Understanding is not about simplification, it's about clarification.
—Richard Saul Wurman

This chapter presents a case study of a manufacturing plant that will be used throughout the remainder of the book to demonstrate the five steps in the transition planning process. To disguise the identity of the particular company I have generalized some of the case study information, although the material is used with permission of the company's planning team. I will refer to the company in the case study as ACME Manufacturing.

FIGURE 4.1
Step One

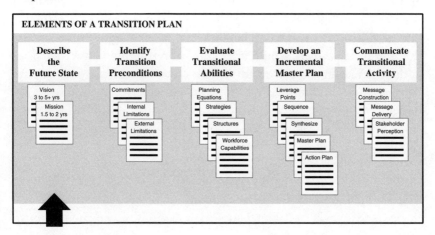

Many planning processes get derailed during the initial step: describing the future state. As a consultant, one of the more difficult activities I am faced with is working with a company that mistakenly believes it has already conducted an adequate planning process, with proper translation and sequencing of work to be accomplished. The client seeks help with the stalled implementation of an initiative, or simply to correct an organization's poor performance. In most cases, the planning process itself was flawed. Managers found themselves at odds in defining what needed to be accomplished and got lost in the sequence of doing what needed to be done. The purpose of describing the future state is to provide clarity of direction—the management team, to the best of their ability, must articulate where the organization is going and what it is ultimately trying to accomplish. This activity combines intuition, experience, and hard data to help management produce an overall guiding document.

There are two steps to defining the future state: identifying a vision and mission statement. Both of these steps would rarely be performed by the same transition planning team. Generally, one vision statement should be sufficient for an organization. Then each division or business unit would create a mission statement using the organizational vision for context. Business units within divisions would also create mission statements within the context of the division's mission statement, within the context of the organization's vision statement. This approach is not always appropriate. For example, a holding company would typically have a vision statement for the parent entity—most likely focused on types of investments and acquisitions to make. Then, each discrete organization within the holding company would create a vision statement, and divisions and units within the organization, mission statements. Some organizations, though identified as corporations legally, have multiple, independent, or unrelated businesses. This usually requires the divisions to create vision statements for their portion of the enterprise.

The Vision Statement

The vision should describe the destiny of the organization at least three to five years out. For some organizations, given the nature of their markets, multiple visions may be in order, projecting the course of the organization five, ten, fifteen years or longer.

If you were to examine 50 vision statements from different organizations, you would immediately notice that their formats are all over the map. Many would be 10, 20, or 30 pages long. I would challenge you to observe how these various organizations translate their visions into action. The more convoluted and voluminous the vision statement, the less likely a clear translation will occur in the organization. It is not necessary to articulate the vision of the company to the *n*th degree. This may cull out creative, intuitive, and innovative aspects of the company's direction. It is, however, necessary to articulate the vision coherently enough so that others outside the planning team understand the vision, and more importantly, so that the vision can be translated into specific strategies, structures, and workforce capabilities (step three in the planning process) for deployment. It's great to have a dynamic, exciting, slogan for a vision, but if it is too vague to translate, it is unlikely the organization will actually ever rally around it.

A vision statement consists of one to two paragraphs which describes the organization's overall intent to stakeholders, including the company's employees.

The vision statement brings together the six to ten key elements that describe the overarching purpose, directives, and critical goals of the organization. In the broadest sense, these elements should comprise a complete definition and a context of the organization and what it is trying to accomplish.

In order to craft an effective vision statement, a corporation must rely on several sources of information, including:

- in-depth interviews with stakeholders
- benchmarking and expert input
- external customer surveys
- internal customer/employee surveys
- competitive/strategic analysis
- existing planning documents
- intuition and experience of the planning team

How much information is enough? The planning team should have a good gut feel about whether enough information and insight is available to draft a vision statement. Planning is iterative; if you discover additional information is needed later on, that's alright. It will not be difficult to incorporate into the plan, as long as the planning team is flexible. This is not an exact science, and trying to make it one is at cross purposes with the realities that constantly reshape organizations.

To begin, have planning participants complete the vision questionnaire described below. Note: This same questionnaire is used for creating the mission statement.

12 Strategic Business Questions*

1. What business should we be in?
2. Why do we exist (what is our basic purpose)?
3. What is unique or distinctive about our organization?
4. Who are our principal customers, clients, or users?
5. What are our principal products and/or services, present, and future?
6. What are our principal market segments, present, and future?
7. What are our principal outlets/distribution channels, present, and future?
8. What is different about our business now from what it was between three and five years ago?
9. What is likely to be different about our business three to five years in the future?
10. What are our principal economic concerns, and how are they measured?
11. What philosophical issues are important to our organization's future?
12. What special considerations do we have in regard to stakeholders (owners, stockholders, investors, constituents, board of directors, parent organization, legislative bodies, employees, customers, clients, users, suppliers, general public, and others)?

Consolidate the data generated for each of the questions. Discuss and clarify the summarized data for each of the questions. By vot-

---

*Source: *The Executive Guide to Strategic Planning* by Patrick J. Below, George L. Morrisey, and Betty L. Acomb. San Francisco: Jossey-Bass Copyright © 1987. Reproduced with permission.

ing or discussion, determine what will be most critical for the organization to accomplish in the next three to five years (typical time frame for vision statements). I usually give each participant six green sticky dots and have them indicate the most critical area of emphasis, and two red dots to indicate the least critical area to focus. Together, the group's green dots will identify six to ten key areas of focus. Note: All of the data identified is important and will ultimately be addressed in the planning process. The vision must address the critical focus.

Next, reach consensus on six to ten vision statement elements. Make sure each element is an actively worded sentence–adding enough substance so that a reader not part of the planning team will understand its intent. For example, a critical area of focus might be corporate assets. Actively worded, this critical area of focus becomes: "Protect and enhance the corporation's assets." Vision elements should have a three- to five-year orientation or longer. This is the major differentiating factor between the vision and the mission statement.

Finally, in subgroups, craft a 15 to 30 word "umbrella" vision statement that conveys the overall meaning of the vision elements and would be understandable by virtually anyone. A well-constructed umbrella statement should be short enough to be placed on the back of a business card. Keeping the vision statement to 30 words can be difficult, but make every effort. The longer the statement the less likely that employees will understand and be able to articulate it—this includes the planning team! Note that the vision umbrella statement is crafted after the strategic elements have been identified. To do this, highlight the key words and phrases in the vision elements. Have subgroups then try to craft an overarching paragraph or two that captures the essence of what is set forth in the vision elements.

Figure 4.2 is an example of a vision statement created by the ACME Manufacturing legal department. The corporate vision statement was not available for publication.

Vision statements created at this point are only in draft form until the organization's stakeholders have had an opportunity to contribute to and validate the effort. Stakeholders might include, but are not limited to, employees, suppliers, customers, stockholders, and other managers and professionals that influence or will be

FIGURE 4.2
Example of a Vision Statement

ACME Manufacturing Vision Statement
Legal Department

Umbrella
Statement ➡

We deliver efficient, quality legal services world-wide consistent with the corporate value statement. Working closely with our customers, we offer independent advice, education and analysis applying broad-based legal and business considerations.

In order to achieve this vision, we will:
- protect and enhance the corporation's assets.
- provide and manage quality professional services while maintaining the highest ethical standards.

Seven Vision
Elements ➡

- maintain a small, efficient and adequately staffed department with global coverage and focus.
- render independent, legal and business advice based on in-depth involvement with business units.
- establish appropriate procedures to comply with laws and company policies; create training programs to improve awareness and knowledge of legal issues and requirements.
- facilitate the continuous evolution of the company's businesses.
- adapt our services to an increasingly international legal/business context.

---

influenced by the end product. This type of real-time feedback is typically eliminated from the planning loop, resulting in a statement that is esoteric and superficial—reality-tested only after it has been adopted and put into action. It is unlikely that this kind of vision will ever be realized. Stakeholders must buy into the plan as it is being developed. If you share your plan with stakeholders after it is completely developed it is likely to overwhelm them no matter how reasonable and logical it is. It will simply be too much information for any reasonable person to grasp all at once. Better to head this entire scenario off before it begins. Get stakeholder buy-in along the way!

Vision statements that are expressed only in conceptual terms tend to be too esoteric for people further down in the organization to relate to, and too vague to ultimately translate into action. An example of a conceptual statement would be, "We want to . . . be a world class manufacturer of widgets. . . ." A vision of this nature becomes very difficult to translate into action unless it is supported with the specific intent the planners had in mind. In this process, the intent is identified in the vision elements. As more people get involved in creating derivative plans (for lower level business units) the true meaning and intent of the vision will not be lost.

The following are some common reasons organizations have difficultly creating vision statements with the necessary degree of concreteness:

- The organization's senior ranks are not really sure of their direction.
- The visioning (creating the vision statement) process is flawed.
- The visioning process is fear-driven, that is, the organization already has a viable vision, but management thinks there must be something wrong with it because performance is sagging.
- Those involved in visioning lack the necessary experience (An infusion of outside perspective and input may help to correct this problem).

These are not reasons to abort the planning process. But they are indicators that the organization will have great difficulty maintaining clarity and focus, and the transition planning process will likely become diluted; quite possibly miss its mark altogether.

It is common for transitioning organizations to have great difficulty in determining direction, or creating a vision statement. Statements about end products are often ambiguous and loaded with value statements that give few clues about the tangible aspects of the future state. Several years ago in a Midwest metal fabrication plant,

I observed this scene: The group of senior executives had given it their best shot. All nine of them had taken a four-hour flight to a beautiful resort area, where they had punished themselves by being locked away in a conference room for three days trying to construct a vision statement for their troubled company. No one was really sure of the results. The CEO said, "Well, I think we are on the right track. It's an evolutionary thing, you know." Other executives were not so forgiving. "This is BS, we can't really make up our minds which way we want to go. I'm not sure how important this visioning stuff is right now anyway. We've got to get our performance up or the vision won't be worth the paper it's written on."

Does this story ring true? Let me continue. The executives return. The draft vision is circulated around to various select groups in the company for feedback. One thing is certain, most people who review the vision statement don't understand it. One division vice president said, "I'm not sure how this vision statement is any different from what we're already doing. It doesn't answer many of the serious organizational and business questions that we are grappling with right now."

The key to constructing a vision statement that can work for your organization lies in making it specific enough. If the vision is not clearly articulated in terms of strategy, structure, and workforce capability, then it is too vague. It must be easy to translate into finite, concrete, actionable objectives and tasks. It is one thing for the CEO and the executive group to have a vision of the future which is esoteric and conceptual in nature. But a vision of this kind is of little value to the workforce and makes little or no contribution to the transition effort. It tends to confuse, even exacerbate an already confusing transitional work environment.

In many, many organizations, business units and divisions simply don't plan because they are waiting for a corporate level vision statement to be created that provides context. It is a reasonable expectation. On more than one occasion, I have had both division and business unit managers say to me that they do not want to invest in planning until the company provides some direction. So what can they do in the meantime? Create a plan anyway and invite the main stakeholders to provide input and approval as the plan is developed. In this way, a business unit or a division can provide leadership for the company.

If you can't create a vision because it is difficult to determine where the company might be three to five years down the road, don't gridlock the planning process over creating a vision. Instead, forget the vision and move on to the mission statement. The mission is really just a vision statement for the short term. Commit the planning group to a course of action in which the visioning process will be revisited at a later time, maybe in 6 months or so. At that time, additional information or an outside perspective may be available, allowing the planning team to see the future more clearly.

If you are leading a business unit you may not need a vision statement. This is especially true if your division or the corporation has done a good job describing a higher-level one. You might ask, "What about planning models that ask you to create a series of separate documents, such as beliefs, objectives, purpose, values, vision, strategies, and mission? I believe that too many of these documents force transition planning into a meaningless, paper-generating exercise. And then you are faced with the task of how to integrate all these documents. The format suggested here rejects some of the traditional planning exercises, replacing them with a few integrated governing documents. I don't isolate the organization's values and purpose because these concepts should be integrated into the vision and mission by using the process set forth here.

The Mission Statement

The second step in describing the future state is to craft a mission statement that is more concrete and specific than the vision statement. It provides a platform from which you can operationalize your organizational goals. The mission statement generally covers a span of 18 to 24 months. In markets where the dynamics shift quickly and there is a constant urgency to change, a mission statement for as little as 6 months may be appropriate. Regardless of the intended life span of this document, it is critical that it be kept alive by incorporating it into the working fabric of the organization. This won't happen unless it is specific and logical and can be translated into the tasks that drive the organization's daily work.

The mission statement, like the vision statement, consists of six to ten key elements. The main difference is that the mission statement answers the question, "What are we going to do right now?"

while the vision statement focuses on the next three to five years. The other important difference is that the vision usually covers the whole corporation, while missions are tailored to individual divisions or units.

The mission statement is structured the same way as the vision statement. Like the vision, it can be used to convey a clear message to people outside the organization, such as customers and stockholders. Everyone in the division or unit organization should be able to repeat it as a mantra of sorts, giving them something to rally around.

The mission statement is created by following the same steps outlined earlier for creating a vision statement. Mission statements are tactical in nature because of their shorter time frame (18 to 24 months) and are oriented to the specific needs of a division or a unit within a division.

Figure 4.3 is an example of a mission statement created by ACME Manufacturing, a division of a Fortune 500 company. It contains an umbrella statement and seven mission statement elements. Note that the umbrella statement exceeds the recommended 15 to 30 word format, but it still appeared to work well with this particular group.

As indicated in Figure 4.4, it is unlikely that the organization's mission and vision statements will be in complete alignment. That is, some of the shorter-term activity the organization must engage in to meet current business demands may cause the organization to veer off its direct path toward the future vision. This explains a common dilemma most organizations face: Short-term activity that must be performed to stay in business is different from the longer-term activity that helps the organization attain its ultimate vision. A good example of this is when a manufacturing organization must invest in equipment that is already obsolete and must be phased out in several years. Management knows that the future demands high-speed equipment, but today's facilities and employee skills are not ready to accommodate the new equipment. Since current customer demand requires quantity, the manufacturer is forced into an interim equipment purchase which is considered less than optimal in view of the long-range vision.

If you have conducted this much of the planning process without losing its integrity, congratulations are in order. Many organiza-

FIGURE 4.3
Example of a Mission Statement

ACME Manufacturing Mission Statement

Umbrella
Statement ➡

ACME will be a world class manufacturer of widgets providing our customers with the best product value anywhere in the world. This will enable us to meet corporate profitability and on-time delivery targets.

The key factors in our success will be continuous improvement, statistically controlled and capable processes, and the empowerment of employees in a team structure.

In order to achieve this mission, we will:

Seven Mission
Elements ➡

- strive for continuous improvement at all levels.
- reduce costs to enable ACME to meet corporate profitability targets.
- have statistically controlled, capable and documented processes ($Cpk \geq 1.33$).
- use a team approach to continuously improve job satisfaction and productivity.
- develop "focussed factories" and use progressive work design.
- be a global supplier of quality products.
- quickly respond to appropriate customer needs through adaptable manufacturing.

---

tions simply cannot, or will not, reach this stage. But this is only the beginning. The vision and/or mission is not yet properly anchored in the organization's environment. In Chapter 5, we will look closely at the realities of the present work environment and use what we find to temper our plan before proceeding. I call this second step "Identifying Transition Preconditions."

FIGURE 4.4
Alignment of Company Vision and Mission

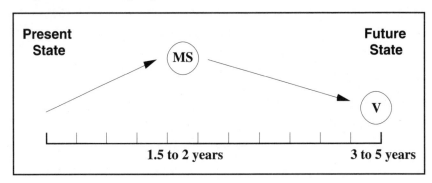

Summary Steps

Creating the Vision Statement

1. The planning team should compile, refresh, or in some cases develop data for the following areas. It is important that prior to creating the vision statement current information is available in these areas and the planning team has had an opportunity to thoroughly review it:
   • in-depth interviews with stakeholders
   • benchmarking and expert input
   • external customer surveys
   • internal customer/employee surveys
   • competitive/strategic analysis
   • existing planning documents
   • intuition and experience of the planning team

2. As prework for a planning meeting, have each participant answer the 12 strategic business questions listed on page XXX. Ask participants to express their ideas in short bulleted sentences which use a noun and a verb (complete sentences tend to be more understandable by others). It is best to have participants use 3 x 5 yellow note cards with sticky backs and express one thought per card. This will facilitate sorting later on.

3. With the planning team assembled, have participants place their responses to the strategic questions on 12 easel sheets, each labeled with one of the strategic questions.

4. Sort the cards on each sheet into like groupings and place headers on each grouping.
5. Thoroughly discuss all groupings of information on all easel sheets. It is acceptable to resort and reorganize the groupings and headers until the group reaches agreement.
6. Give each participant six green sticky dots. Ask them to place their dots on headers which represent the most critical areas of focus for the next three to five years (or a longer duration if appropriate).
7. Give each participant two red sticky dots. Ask them to place these dots on headers which represent the least critical areas of focus or those which might even be counterproductive to the organization's success over the next three to five years. This voting is elective—participants may choose not to use the red dots.
8. Tabulate the dots. Each green dot counts as +1 and each red dot counts as –1.
9. Based on the scoring, identify the six to ten critical focal areas. These are the vision statement elements.
10. Refine each of the elements into sentences (actively worded and with enough substance so that a reader who is not part of the planning team will understand its intent) which will logically follow a phrase such as: "In order to achieve this, we will:", "We do this by:" or "The key factors to our success will be:"
11. Craft a 15- to 30-word umbrella statement that conveys the overall meaning of the vision elements. Do this by highlighting key words and phrases in elements and then drafting an overarching statement that includes as many of these key points as possible. Note: It will be difficult to keep this statement to 15 to 30 words. However, the longer the statement, the less likely it is a clear, understandable, and rememberable expression of vision.
12. Review the draft vision statement with stakeholders. Revise the document, as appropriate, from input.

Creating the Mission Statement

The mission statement is created in the same format as the vision statement. The data for this document will tend to be more specific because the time frame is 18 to 24 months, not three to five years.

To create a mission statement, follow the steps as outlined above. One additional data point for the planning team will be the vision statement of the organization. During steps six and seven above, vote with the sticky dots on critical areas of focus for the next 18 to 24 months. Note: Given the nature of the division or business unit, a shorter time frame for the mission may be appropriate.

Review the draft mission statement with stakeholders including the planning team participants which developed the company's vision statement. Revise as appropriate.

5

Identify Transition Preconditions

Only that which is provisional endures.
—French Proverb

Transition preconditions are the commitments and limitations that could impede successful change. If they are not acknowledged and addressed proactively, you can bet that some unaccounted aspect of them will appear at an inopportune time and either derail the planning process or render the plan impotent somewhere down the road. Preconditions must be identified at the beginning of the planning process to be managed effectively. It is a relatively easy task to identify and list those things that influence and shape the organization's direction.

FIGURE 5.1
Step Two

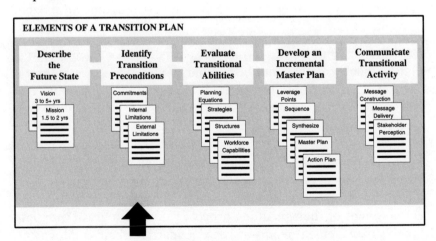

The following is a list of commitments and limitations identified by the ACME Manufacturing's divisional planning team. It includes corporate, division, customer, and competitor requirements across the two categories. The ACME planning team believed that, at minimum, any plan they concocted had to take into account these commitments and limitations if it were to be successfully implemented:

Commitments

- On time delivery should be 92 percent by year end.
- Must meet SG&A cost reduction targets of 3 percent.
- Must achieve business volume target of 900,000 units.
- Need to fully implement the Quality Improvement system adopted by the division.
- Must meet corporate and division goals for 25 percent of sales from new products.
- Must meet ISO 9000 certification (international quality standards for manufacturing).

Limitations

- On average, workforce has low educational attainment.
- Management/structural changes for worldwide division are unsettled.
- Moving toward team structure with reduced levels of management.
- Project commitments demand significant resources.
- All plans affecting staffing levels, and training and development of employees must be reviewed and approved by European labor committees.

Although some of the terminology used by this manufacturing management team may not be familiar to you, what is important is that this team's planning process did take into account important and necessary commitments and limitations for their own survival. The corporation believes that there are certain requirements their manufacturing divisions must meet in order to stay competitive. For example, ISO 9000 certification is a requirement because their customer base demands the company meet this standard for manufacturing quality. To not acknowledge ISO 9000 as an implicit commitment of their planning process would be a grave oversight for this management team—it could jeopardize their employment.

FIGURE 5.2
Transition Preconditions Clarification and Identification

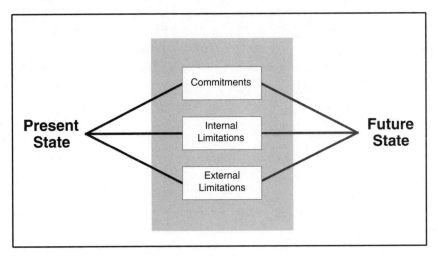

Figure 5.2 shows three categories of preconditions that must be identified and clarified.

It is not my purpose here to name all of the preconditions you and your planning team might encounter. But I can help to prime the pump. The alert planning team recognizes that preconditions are not necessarily obvious. It will require a good deal of effort to ferret them out, but this effort will pay handsomely in the long run. The excitement begins when you present your preconditions list to your stakeholders and ask if they agree with what you have come up with. You will probably discover that various stakeholders will surprise you. Some of the preconditions you thought important are inconsequential to them, while they will probably identify other critical preconditions that are not even on your list. Eventually these preconditions may considerably alter the vision and mission statements described in the future state.

Organizational Commitments

Commitments are specific agreements, such as business goals. There are several types of commitments to look for and carefully consider in developing the transition preconditions list.

First, there is a range of official or formal commitments. These are commitments that are well documented and communicated, such as return on investment (ROI) goals, dollars in sales growth, and expansion plans. For example, it would not be unusual to see a directive issued from top management requiring: achieve a 1.0 return on assets (ROA) by end of fiscal year and the reduction of full time employees (FTE) by 15 percent prior to the end of the third quarter. Many of these directives are issued outside the context of a transition plan, but must be honored even in the midst of massive organizational transition.

It is quite possible that numerous official commitments are floating around the organization, many unknown to interested or affected parties. For example, the annual report of a hospital conglomerate noted a target to reduce its nosocomial infection rate (hospital acquired diseases). Planning teams in some of the affiliated hospitals were unaware of this goal. This is a typical symptom of a broken down communication system in an organization in transition. These official and formal commitments must be discovered and included on the preconditions list because inevitably they will be an important criterion to someone in the organization—someone's performance will be measured against them.

A second type of commitment is one that is pledged. A pledged commitment might be a circumstance in which a manager is promoted to clean up a division or go after a certain financial objective. Pledges are difficult to uncover because of their informal and sometime secretive nature. Yet if you ask the planning team to name pledged commitments they know of, you might be surprised by the number and variety that surface.

The third type of commitment might be classified as personal values. A simple rule in transition management: Don't ask people to do something that goes against their values and beliefs—or their emotional commitments. It is a sure formula for disaster. An example of a personal value commitment might be "to reduce the use of fluorocarbons in our manufacturing processes to protect the earth's ozone layer." Until recently, this was more of an individual cause than a societal one. This can put many individuals at odds with employers not committed to the environment and reducing fluorocarbon use.

A final type of commitment might be called the ultimate agenda or hidden agenda. Few managers engage in a transition planning process without bringing with them a list of issues they would like to see changed or done differently in the company. If these managers don't put these issues on the table early on, they may have to be forced into the plan later. One CEO's ultimate agenda included:

- Every out-source provider must use some form of statistical process control to monitor parts production.
- All major initiatives (management training, new sales reporting system, TQM) must be coordinated and administered within the context of the transition plan.
- Every business unit must work from a business plan.
- Zero-based budgeting is the norm, not the exception.
- Opportunities for cooperation among divisions in the use of materials, equipment, and so forth, are identified and promoted.
- Common performance guidelines are clearly defined and measured for all employees, regardless of level, in order to raise accountability in the company.

Looking again at the example of ACME Manufacturing, prior to the division's planning activity, the company had created a model of world class manufacturing through benchmarking and expert input. It was decided by executive management that the company's manufacturing divisions should begin to migrate toward the characteristics identified in this model. It became part of the planning team's ultimate agenda. Figures 5.3 through 5.5, the benchmark model, serve as another planning reference point, which has been described in terms of strategies, structures, and workforce capability.

Desired organizational characteristics, as noted in these benchmark models, when incorporated into the planning process will ultimately help gauge the possibility of achieving them and the size and duration of the task at hand.

Organizational Limitations

Another dimension of transition preconditions stems from organizational limitations. Organizations have a very specific and obvious set of limitations that are inherent in their strategies, structures, and workforce capabilities. The point of identifying limiters is not to create a self-fulfilling defeatist prophecy, but rather to come to

FIGURE 5.3
Benchmark Model—Strategies

Strategies to Attain World Class Manufacturing Status

Achieve 99+Percent Delivery Performance
• flexible equipment

Be Lower Cost Producer
• high return on assets
• continuously reduced costs
• no WIP (work in progress backlogs)
• continuous flow manufacturing

Improve by Benchmarking
• periodically refresh and increase skill and knowledge

Six Σ Quality
• consistent products (aesthetics)
• consistent quality of products

Master Time Based Competition
• short cycle time as a competitive weapon
• rapid scale-up of new products

Adapt Easily to Changing Needs
• customer responsive
• flexible manufacturing

---

grips with those influencers that genuinely define what an organization can do or simply isn't capable of doing.

Limitations stem from a variety of sources. An example of an employee limitation could be low literacy levels. In many manufacturing businesses, production employees with minimal skills have been hired for menial, repetitive tasks. Now requirements have been placed on manufacturers for cost, production, and quality improvement, requiring employees to have more advanced levels of math and English skills. For example, Statistical Process Control

FIGURE 5.4
Benchmark Model—Structures

Structures to Attain World Class Manufacturing Status

Flatten Organization Structure
• fewer management levels

Expand Training System
• excellent training and certification in place

Develop Real Time Information Systems
• effectively used Materials Resource Planning (MRP)
• shop floor scheduling
• integrated business/operating/financial plans (MRP II)
• daily ship performance
• real time data analysis
• data driven, not opinions

Implement Total Productive Maintenance, Activity Based Costing and Visual Factory
• Kanban systems

Excel in Process Control
• standardized processes
• capable processes (Cpk of 2 or better)
• standard processes
• in-line QC
• documentation for all processes (mfg., systems, planning)
• data acquisition and process control everywhere
• automated processes where feasible

Reinforce Customer Supplier Partnership
• broad measure of customer satisfaction on regular basis

Pay for Performance
• gain sharing

FIGURE 5.5
Benchmark Model—Workforce Capability

Workforce Capability to Attain World Class Manufacturing Status

Increase Employee Satisfaction
• enthusiastic workforce / satisfied employees
• everyone understands vision, mission
• excellent communication - no secrets

Implement Continuous Improvement (CI) At All Levels

Facilitate Team Work
• self-directed teams
• egalitarian

Develop Highly Skilled Staff
• highly skilled (math, computers, CI, production, scheduling)
• technician type operators
• excellent technical support, well integrated w/ floor

Empower Workforce
• committed, well-trained workforce

(SPC), a management tool used to control the tolerances and general quality of manufacturing processes, simply cannot be performed by a workforce without a minimal level of literacy. Launching an SPC initiative prematurely, prior to teaching employees the necessary reading and writing skills, would be a wasteful endeavor.

Limitations affect the speed with which organizations are able to assimilate and deploy new processes and systems. This is especially true in organizations attempting to install complex processes and systems that place heavy demands on the workforce. For example, high performance and self-directed work teams are hybrid and complex organizational systems that often are implemented long before organizational limitations are addressed, dooming the implementation to eventual failure.

I typically ask groups to think about two types of limitations: those inherent in the organization (internal limitations) and those imposed on the organization from outside sources (external limitations). Here are some examples of both types of these limitations:

Internal Limitations

- Employee skill level.
- Product capability—The organization does not have the expertise to perform certain types of fabrication activities used by competition.
- Manufacturing capacity—Given space constraints and current equipment configurations, manufacturing volume cannot achieve desired levels.
- Systems capability—Current systems are limited and will not generate necessary reports.
- Geography—The organization is not physically positioned to best serve emerging customers domestically and abroad.
- Corporate culture—An organization's values may prevent its competing in certain markets (e.g., China because of human rights violations).

External Limitations

- Competitive pricing—A larger or more efficient organization can offer lower prices.
- Customer demands—Customers have imposed standards on you that require you to conform if you want to do business with them. For instance, customers are demanding that their suppliers adopt TQM practices. This may also be identified as a formal commitment.
- Market trends—The market is moving away from your product to a newer technology or service.
- Government regulation—Both domestic and foreign excise taxes make a particular market unattractive.
- New competition—Entry of new competitors limit market potential.

Summary Steps

The foregoing types of transition preconditions are not all inclusive. You must identify all the various preconditions peculiar to your organization that might impede the development of an implementable or achievable transition plan. A finalized transition plan should always be reviewed against this preconditions list to make sure that all points have been adequately addressed and that conscious decisions have been made about which commitments to pursue, and which limitations to overcome.

1. Before a transition planning meeting, have each planning team member brainstorm items for commitments, internal limitations, and external limitations.
2. Consolidate and discuss these lists in the transition planning meeting.
3. Identify stakeholders (managers, board of director members, and employees) outside the transition planning team to review the consolidated list. Stakeholders identified for this activity should be few in number and should respect the confidential nature of this information.
4. Use this information as input in the next step, evaluate transitional abilities.

6

Evaluate Transitional Abilities

It requires a very unusual mind to undertake the analysis of the obvious.
—Alfred North Whitehead

Imagine that you are in total darkness. You know that the pillar you are standing on will collapse in the near future and there is another pillar somewhere in your vicinity. Your mission is to jump to the next pillar before the one you are standing on collapses. Missing this jump could cost you your life. Ready to jump? Of course not. You need additional information before you can confidently make that all-important leap. Knowing where you want to land (your future state) is simply not enough information to make your jump successful. You first need to answer some critical questions. What is your jumping ability? How far and how high can you jump? Can you jump these distances consistently? Is there a particular jumping technique in which you excel? When is the best time to make the jump? Together, the answers to these questions describes your organization's transitional ability.

In the context of a business transition, evaluating your transitional ability represents the present reality of your organization—its capabilities, capacities, strengths, and weaknesses. The future state, the next pillar you must jump to in order to survive and remain a viable organization, represents the second reference point; the landing point. A thorough understanding of the distance between these two points is the real key to a successful organizational transition. By evaluating this information in light of the transition preconditions you identified earlier (to keep you grounded in reality) you can begin to mold the heart of a transition plan.

FIGURE 6.1
Step Three

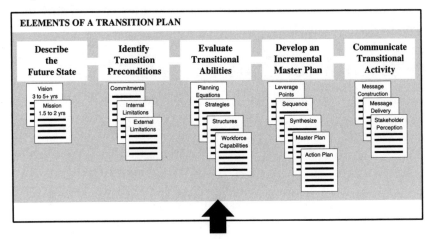

It is common practice for a management team to invest several days in creating vision and mission statements, two critical components of the future state, and then to try to operationalize them in the work environment without addressing the sometimes dramatic gaps between the proposed plan and the organization's capabilities. It is at this point that planning may disintegrate in several ways:

- commitment to transition activities that far exceed the organization's systems, processes and workforce capabilities
- too many priorities and confusion regarding which should be addressed first
- an unrealistic timetable and budget for achieving future state objectives which outpaces the workforce's ability to assimilate it
- a plan that is difficult to break down into small incremental pieces

Only with a clear definition of your organization's present resources and abilities can you determine the most effective path to the future goals. During the transitional abilities analysis, it usually becomes apparent that:

1. Most aspects of the organization will not need to be altered dramatically in the short term.
2. Some aspects of the transition need immediate attention.

3. Some aspects of the desired change require significant departures from how the organization is accustomed to operating. Their implementation will require careful discovery, education, and benchmarking.
4. Many skills ingrained in the organization's workforce may have little or no relevance to the future state.

Let's take a look at each of these points in greater depth.

1. Most Aspects of the Organization Will Not Need To Be Altered Dramatically in the Short Term

It is not atypical for organizations to become fixated on change; in fact, to set off a frenzy of change. If it is old, it must be bad and there must be a new, better and dramatically different way of doing it. This approach to transition is based on the wrong logic. If too many things were dramatically wrong or dysfunctional in the organization, it couldn't manufacture products or provide services—there would not be a business to worry about transitioning. For example, Dr. Jay W. Forrester, MIT professor and designer of the SAGE national security communications system, noted that when the system was developed (late 1950s), computers used vacuum tubes. Each SAGE communication station (multiple locations throughout the United States) used about 50,000 vacuum tubes in its computer equipment. Even though vacuum tube technology was replaced with solid state components two decades before the centers were refitted, the computers were left alone—outmoded vacuum technology and all. The reason? The system had 99.9 percent up-time for the 30 years it was in operation. Had the system and its performance not been carefully analyzed, it would have been unnecessarily replaced.

Chances are that many of your organization's processes, systems, strategies, and workforce capabilities may need to be updated or altered, but not in a radical way. At least not within the next six months, or even a year. Research by the Dallas, Texas, based research and consulting firm Prichett & Associates, Inc., suggests that average worker productivity drops to 45 percent during transition from a normal average of 73 percent. What does this tell us? When managing a transition, don't slow down to do it right; rather speed up and make the transition efficient. Make sure that when you disrupt employee routines you have something to replace them—and a plan for making the changes.

A careful study of the transitional abilities of the organization is important because we want to make sure to change only that which needs changing. Many times it is prudent to have an outside consultant participate in this analysis. A different set of eyes can usually see the competent behavior that permeates most organizations. But do not go so far as to have the consultant actually perform the analysis. It is important not to relegate or delegate away any aspect of the transition planning process, as the process serves as much to educate and develop the transition team as to create a logical path to the future.

2. Some Aspects of the Transition Need Immediate Attention

Routine tends to mask priorities. Behaviors that have existed in the environment long-term, or have evolved in the environment over time, can be dangerous, ineffective, or costly and badly in need of change. For example, a manufacturing organization may never measure their machine output accurately. No controls are in place. Here is an opportunity to improve efficiency and profitability, which should be a number one priority. Accurate data regarding how well you are actually doing (cause and effect) is critical information to the transition planning process. Let's make sure we know how well we are doing and why we are doing that well (or poorly) before deciding to change something. This is where a lot of clues can be found regarding what areas of the organization might need immediate attention. ACME manufacturing collected customer complaint data going back two years looking for process and systems issues. The complaints revealed that there was nothing dramatically wrong with the main order entry system, the only problem was how it was being used.

A dramatic example of a competitor-triggered transition needing immediate attention occurred several years ago in the food retailing industry. Consumer mind-set has changed dramatically over the last ten years with the help of some competitive practices. Lucky Food Stores began a campaign to win over customers frustrated by long lines. Besides offering a low price, they promoted a slogan: "Never more than three in line." The impact of this campaign was dramatic on competitors not oriented to providing this type of quick turnaround service. It went far beyond adequate staffing for line surges to inventory and checkout technology (to improve transaction efficiency). An entire reorientation to the concepts of customer service was needed. As a result, customers have learned to expect to be treated as the number one priority at all points of contact with a service organization.

As an interesting aside, customers began transferring the no more than three in line concept introduced by Lucky Food Stores to other industries. Within months, some banks located in the same geography began receiving complaints when more than three people were in line.

If urgent transitional activities exist and need immediate attention, why are they ignored or postponed by many businesses? For several reasons. They are not glamorous. They have existed in the environment for so long that they have become almost invisible. Workers are not sure exactly how to approach and fix them. The value of fixing these processes or behaviors is not known.

Management teams may respond to the urgency of transition by taking some significant actions that are highly visible, trendy, and acclaimed in the business community. They believe this proves that they are responsive and on top of things. But this type of activity only derails the organization because the transition is based on a weak foundation.

Let me be clear that I am not opposed to the major, popular undertakings most organizations have engaged in: leadership development, total quality management, high performance work teams, world class manufacturing. Yet, there is a logical sequence to what and how much an organization can absorb. Each organization has its own sequence, its own critical path, that it must identify for an efficient, effective transition. As a transition planning team evaluates its organization and talks with stakeholders, it frequently reorders its priorities. Priority setting will be discussed in Chapter 7.

3. Some Aspects of the Desired Change Require Significant Departures from How the Organization is Accustomed to Operating. Their Implementation will Require Careful Discovery, Education and Benchmarking

A change in competition or market conditions can trigger a need for new manufacturing or service techniques. Sometimes these required changes can be so radically different from current practice that an incremental step or evolutionary step won't suffice. For example, based on demands from international markets, a food processing and packing house needed to supplement its line with freeze-dried products. Most aspects of this technology are not new, but application to their product type was. The company needed extensive exploration and education to determine how to enter this new market.

Organizations that have been successful in installing TQM have a track record of careful discovery, education, and benchmarking. Organizations that struggle or fail to institute TQM are those that do not have the patience and tenacity to engage in a difficult, extended new learning experience. A midwest manufacturing firm decided to pursue TQM. After careful investigation the management team learned that the company was not organized to deliver the level of quality their customer base was beginning to expect. Based on educational seminars, benchmarking, and competitive analysis, they surmised that the company was organized incorrectly, from the executive suites right down to the factory floor and that they were not adequately skilled in, or even aware of, some new technologies necessary to create total quality. This discovery and realization helped them form an approach that was comprehensive enough to address their needs.

4. Many Skills Ingrained in the Organization's Workforce May Have Little or No Relevance to the Future State

Skill depreciation occurs in almost every transition. This means that workforce skills and knowledge will not be completely aligned with the new tasks at hand. General capabilities need to be enhanced and replaced by more updated ones. For example, when the fabrication process is modified in a manufacturing plant, workers may find themselves unable to perform the new job without extensive training. Current capabilities are no longer enough to get the job done. With deregulation, banking employees experienced severe skill depreciation. Skills shifted from loan order taker and applicant screener to that of selling financial services, sometimes out of the branch office. This shift in job demand has been such a radical departure from the traditional banker's role that tremendous turnover has resulted. Virtually all banking institutions experienced a similar skill deficit problem so no competitor immediately had an advantage. A common skill deficit in the white collar ranks occurs with the shift from a command and control to a shared responsibility management style. The command and control management style is a difficult pattern to break. In some instances, it is probably better to move the manager out of the organization or into a single contributor position than continue to invest time and effort in behavior pattern change.

It is important to assess the degree to which your transition plan calls for skills and knowledge that your workforce does not have, as well as the level of education, training and, replacement required to accommodate the needed changes. As transition planners, you have the responsibility for engineering the transition so that the workforce can assimilate required changes and will be able to perform the intended work. The speed with which workers can reasonably be expected to assimilate new information and upgrade performance should be directly proportional to the amount they are expected to change.

What Is a Planning Equation?

With those ground rules established, we're ready to uncover the abilities and resources that an organization will need to reach its future state. Many corporations have found that planning equations are the best tools for identifying the specific steps that link the present state to the future state.

A planning equation consists of a vision or mission element and the supporting strategy, structure and workforce capability required to achieve it. It is one thing for a planning team to discuss strategy. Strategy discussions tend to represent conceptual, long-range ideals and goals. It is not until the strategy, structure and workforce capability, are added in that the conversation comes into clear focus. Each identified strategy has specific associated supporting structure and workforce capability correlates that can help point to where a particular element is likely to take you—which may be disparate with the original intent. As I said in chapter 1, the strategy is a specific course of action necessary to help achieve a vision or mission element; structure refers to the tangibles, such as systems, processes, standards, brick and mortar, policies, proce-

FIGURE 6.2
ACME Manufacturing Planning Equation

Mission element:	Strive for continuous improvement at all levels
Strategy:	Provide adequate staffing for technical support
Structure:	Conduct periodic human resource reviews
WF Capability:	Develop skills necessary to understand CI needs for technical projects

dures, training programs and equipment necessary to support the strategy; workforce capability is made up of the skills, knowledge, attitude, commitment and values necessary to work within a given structure in support of the strategy.

An element of ACME Manufacturing's mission statement in chapter 4 was "Strive for continuous improvement (CI) at all levels." One strategy for accomplishing this element is "Adequate staffing for technical support." The planning equation would be formed when a structure (periodic resource reviews) and a workforce capability (skills necessary to understand CI needs for technical projects) combine in support of the strategy. The main purpose of the planning equation is to fully describe the combined strategy, structure and workforce capability for a given element.

First, each vision or mission element is broken down into its component parts: strategies, structures and workforce capabilities. There can be multiple strategies to accomplish a given element; I recommend that no less than 10 or more than 15 are identified in order to to keep the activity thorough but focused. For each strategy there can be multiple supporting structural components (processes, procedures, policies, work configurations, equipment). Each strategy/structure combination suggests certain skills, knowledge, and commitments that the workforce must have.

In the example that follows, I have shown how a particular element of a vision/mission statement might branch out to strategies, structures, and workforce capabilities.

At first, planning equations may be difficult to create. One partic-

FIGURE 6.3

Flow Diagram of a Planning Equation

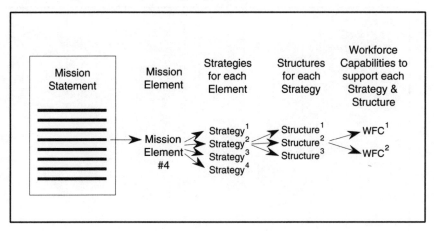

ipant summed it up: "I have never had to think about organizational issues in such a disciplined way." This is precisely the reason planning equations are so useful. The complexity of an organization can be mind-boggling. We need to plan in a systematic way that goes beyond having a conceptual, strategic discussion. Planning equations force the thought process beyond the strategic level to examine the specifics of strategies, structures, and workforce capabilities to develop a very specific plan to address the real complexities of an organization. The equations keep the planning team discussing all aspects of change activities in an integrated fashion; that is, strategies are not set forth in isolation. As a strategy is discussed, so are the organization's structure and the workforce's capabilities.

Figure 6.4 is a sample Transition Planning Worksheet that contains space for three planning equations. There are three vertical sections to the worksheet. The first column is titled Planning Equations. On the first line a vision/mission element is entered, labeled with its assigned number. The second line is labeled Strategy. One possible strategy for achieving the vision/mission element is entered here. On the next line, Structure, a structural component that supports the given strategy is described. The last lines, labeled Workforce Capability, are used to describe a workforce capability component that supports both the strategy and structure listed above it.

FIGURE 6.4
Transition Planning Worksheet

Planning Equations	Preparedness / Importance	Notes
1) Strive for continuous improvement at all levels	A B C D E	Notes
Strategy Adequate staffing for technical support	Strategy	
Structure Periodic, scheduled resource reviews	Structure	
Workforce Capability Skills necessary to understand CI needs for technical projects	Workforce Capability	
	Ranking 2CCB Pend ☐	
1) Strive for continuous improvement at all levels	A B C D E	Notes
Strategy Implement a quality strategy based on Deming philosophy	Strategy	
Structure Workforce organized into manufacturing cells with verticle teams	Structure	
Workforce Capability Develop ability to work in self-directed team environment	Workforce Capability	
	Ranking 1CBA Pend ☐	
( )	A B C D E	Notes
Strategy	Strategy	
Structure	Structure	
Workforce Capability	Workforce Capability	
	Ranking Pend ☐	

Taken together, this results in one planning equation for the element listed. Ten to fifteen planning equations may be generated for a given element. It is important that each equation contain only one combination of strategy, structure, and workforce capability. If more than one strategy is identified for a given element, a new equation is created. If more than one structure is identified for a given strategy of an element, again, a new equation is created—even though the strategy and the workforce capability might be the same. These equations will be prioritized later so don't be afraid now of generating equations with conflicting strategies. The primary purpose of the equations is to provide a comprehensive, systematic format for collecting planning data—if we are to achieve the vision or mission, what are we currently prepared to do and what else will we need to do?

Each vision/mission element would be repeated in an equation until all associated strategies for accomplishing it had been listed. In the example above, "strive for continuous improvement at all levels" is element 1 of ACME Manufacturing's draft mission statement. For each strategy listed, associated structure and workforce capability components would be listed until all are identified in an equation. A tip about how to do this efficiently: Brainstorm a list of all potential strategies for each element. (This is usually done in subgroups as prework to a planning section.) Identify the top three strategies that you feel will make the greatest contribution to achieving the mission element over the next 12 months. Create planning equations for these three strategies first, then add strategies from your list. Do not exceed a total of 10 to 15 planning equations per mission element.

Have the author (or a representative from the subgroup which authored it) present his planning equations. Note: It helps to have transferred the completed worksheets onto overhead transparencies. With group input, modify planning equation language, if needed, to reach agreement on its strategy, structure and workforce capability. The group should challenge reasoning and the appropriateness of activities described in the equation. For example, there is a tendency to put training-related items under workforce capability. This is incorrect. Training requires a program, which is a structure. Items appropriate to list under workforce capability include specific types of skill and knowledge, management commitment necessary to institute a particular strategy, and capabilities necessary to work within the described structure.

Next the equation is ranked on two dimensions: preparedness and importance. Ranking is always done as a team following discussion and modification of the equation's wording, never beforehand. Each change activity is discussed in sufficient detail to allow the planning team to easily determine how prepared the organization is to do it and how important the change is to the overall scheme of things. This makes sequencing, one of the initial activities in master planning, relatively simple and reliable. Traditionally, I have found this to be a difficult and unreliable activity using other analytical formats. Ranking scales for these two dimensions are included in this chapter. The ranking process ties the analysis of the future state to the reality of the present organizational abilities. The ranking represents the planning team's best estimate of the organization's capabilities in the present state that will allow it to move forward into the prescribed future state.

In Figure 6.4, two equations created by the ACME Manufacturing Company are ranked based on preparedness and importance.

Ranking Preparedness

How prepared is the team to implement the planning equation they have described given their current experience, demonstrated organizational capabilities, and existing resources? The Preparedness Scale is used to answer this question. The scale runs from "A" which means no experience and many unknowns, to "E" which translates to "we have a successful track record performing this activity." Note that strategy, structure, and workforce capability, are each graded.

Only after an equation is ranked on preparedness should it be scored on importance. This is done to prevent the importance ranking from influencing the amount of attention given to the content of the equation. For example, an equation receiving a very low importance ranking would not command much preparedness discussion, yet it may wind up as an activity that must be performed early on in the transition because it is a prerequisite for other criti-

FIGURE 6.5
Preparedness Scale

A = No experience. Don't think we are ready to do this. Many unknowns.

Strategy   Strategy is not formulated.

Structure   Structure is not defined (or necessary structure is nonexistent).

Workforce   Skills, knowledge and capabilities necessary to perform this activity are
Capability   absent or not clear.

B = Marginal capability, no direct or related experience. Not sure of our ability to perform this activity.

Strategy   Strategy formulation is incomplete. It is difficult to see how or why we might do this.

Structure   Most aspects of the required structure are unclear. It is obvious that there are gaps in information over what is required.

Workforce   It is apparent that the workforce is not equipped with all of the skills
Capability   and knowledge necessary to perform this task and that external input and training will be necessary.

C = Partial capability, no direct experience. Seems feasible but not completely thought through.

Strategy   The overall strategy and the reasoning behind it are apparent. It is relatively easy to see the logic to do this and how it will be approached.

Structure   Most of the key systems, processes, equipment, etc., necessary to perform this activity are known and appear doable.

Workforce   Some skill and knowledge is required in order to perform this activity.
Capability   No critical skill and knowledge gaps are seen. Some workforce development will be necessary.

D = Some familiarity with subject. Have experience applicable to the requirements of this activity.

Strategy   The strategy is clear and most aspects of it can be easily translated into specifics.

Structure   Most of the structural aspects of this activity are known and have been done before.

Workforce   Workforce is equipped with most skills and knowledge requirements or
Capability   can readily learn them.

E = Have performed before or have experience doing this activity. Have a successful track record with this activity.

Strategy   Strategy is formulated and is very clear and specific.

Structure   Structural components are identified, and how to create, acquire, or logistically position them is known.

Workforce   Workforce currently has the skills and knowledge necessary to support
Capability   the named strategy and structure.

cal activities. An abbreviated discussion could restrict rich and important equation content dialogue at this stage.

Ranking Importance

Regardless of the level of preparedness, how important is this particular planning equation to the transitioning needs of the organization? The Importance Scale is used to answer this question. Level 1 means that the activity (strategy, structure, and workforce capability) should be addressed in the next 6 to 12 months. At the other end of the Importance Scale, a 3 indicates an activity that would be nice to do but investing the resources would be of little benefit over the next year or so. It is critical that the planning team not worry about how many level 1 importance ratings are assigned. It is typical to rank 40 percent to 70 percent of the planning equations as 1 on the Importance Scale. Equations will be consolidated later. Also, don't confuse importance with priority. Sequencing, which is the primary determinant of priority, is discussed in detail in the next chapter.

The Pend box located below the ranking box in Figure 6.4 is used when a planning team can't agree on the strategy, structure, and workforce capability and/or the ranking for an equation. Rather than spend too much time, it is better to pend the equation and address it later if need be.

The notes column on the far right of the Transition Planning form is used to record any details unique to a particular planning

FIGURE 6.6
Importance Scale

1 = Critical to address in next six to twelve months.

2 = Important, but not critical. Not sure how this would make a significant contribution if performed in the next six to twelve months.

3 = Nice to do, but considered lower in importance. If necessary, organization could survive without doing this at all.

equation that might not be conveyed in the equation itself. The note serves as a reminder to the planning team or someone else reviewing the team's work.

The following is a random sample of planning equations from ACME Manufacturing Company. These equations have been included to give you a feel for what completed equations look like and examples of strategies, structures, and workforce capabilities. You will note that the planning equations are no longer in the worksheet format and the mission elements (4, 7, 3, etc.) are in no particular order. The importance and preparedness rankings for each equation are indicated on the lower right-hand side.

4. Use a team approach to continuously improve job satisfaction and productivity.

>   *Strategy*: Increase product/process focus—management commitment to create small team structure.

>   *Structure*: Multifunctional product/process focused cells.

>   *WF Capability*: Workforce capable of working in small teams.

>   *1DCB*

7. Quickly respond to appropriate customer needs through adaptable manufacturing.

>   *Strategy*: Identify and prioritize customer needs.

>   *Structure*: Segregate adaptable manufacturing equipment from standard equipment.

>   *WF Capability*: Teams have knowledge of customer needs.

>   *1BCA*

3. Have statistically controlled, capable, and documented processes (Cpk ≥ 1.33).

>   *Strategy*: Management commitment to relate role/org. changes to pay/progression systems.

>   *Structure*: P&P system which is responsive to changing work environment.

>   *WF Capability*: Employees understand link and accept it.

>   *1CCB*

5. Develop "focused factories" and use progressive work design.

>   *Strategy*: Management commitment to a flatter organization.

>   *Structure*: Accessible information systems.

>   *WF Capability*: All operators have clear systems understanding.

>   *1CBB*

3. Have statistically controlled, capable, and documented process-es (Cpk ≥ 1.33).

 Strategy: Management commitment to use SPC in all processes.

 Structure: SPC data management system.

 WF Capability: Engineer skills to enter/manipulate data.

              1CBB

1. Strive for continuous improvement at all levels.

 Strategy: Top down commitment.

 Structure: Long-term strategy/strategic planning process.

 WF Capability: Consistency of purpose.

              1DBC

3. Have statistically controlled, capable, and documented process-es (Cpk ≥ 1.33).

 Strategy: ISO 9000 certified.

 Structure: Document control system.

 WF Capability: Committed workforce follows, believes pro-cedures, etc.

              1CBB

7. Quickly respond to appropriate customer needs through adapt-able manufacturing.

 Strategy: Flexible manufacturing in print/assemble/pack/label.

 Structure: Systematic link with production management/clear definition of necessary capabilities for marketing needs.

 WF Capability: Appropriate technical knowledge to design/implement technology.

              1CBC

Planning equations provide a format for exploring, in detail, cross-functional work integration. An extended discussion in this format promotes cross-functional alignment. Even if the planning process was stopped and did not continue to the master planning phase, the team would function better because its cross-function perspective had been developed. Using many traditional planning approaches functional areas, sales, manufacturing, engineering, customer service, finance, and human resources create independent plans based on a collaborative vision statement. Close examination of these plans would show that functional areas are inextricably linked and that unintegrated planning at this stage will generate a huge number of top priorities. These invariably compete for resources and can't be accomplished without cross-functional support. For example, a large Midwest insurance company asked each of its seven divisions to present their plans for the next three fiscal years. The divisions performed their planning without participation from several key support organizations. The result: plans not adequately based on reality. The divisions had little idea if the finance, information systems, and human resources corporate support organizations could in fact deliver against the commitments set forth in their plans. Had planning been cross-functional from the beginning, this situation would not have occurred.

At this point in the planning process you will have a general idea about how large the gaps are in strategy, structure, and workforce capability, and between where you are now and where you want to be in the future. You will know the magnitude of your journey to achieve your future state: to what degree the workforce will need to evolve skill and knowledge and current capabilities; levels of capital that may be necessary to make sure that the right equipment, systems and facilities are created. With all of the equations completed and the ranking complete, you have laid the foundation for creating a master plan. This can feel like a let-down to the planning team. Most of the planning work has been done, but it is difficult to see exactly how all of this will come together. Not to worry. Your moment of excitement is close at hand.

Summary Steps

1. Each team member can complete planning equations on all of the vision/mission elements, or specific elements can be assigned to subgroups based on related experience.
2. Working on one vision/mission element at a time, brainstorm a list of possible strategies for achieving that goal.
3. Rank the list of possible strategies and decide on the top three that you think will have the greatest impact if carried out over the next 12 months. Save the list of other strategies that were brainstormed to see if they get covered in some other area.

4. Using Transition Planning worksheets, finish the planning equation for the top three strategies by defining at least one structure and one workforce capability component necessary to effectively implement the strategy. It is likely that it will take two or more structure and workforce capability components to effectively carry out each strategy. Repeat the strategy component in as many equations as necessary in order to fully document the structure and workforce capability components associated with it.

   Important note. *A general rule for creating planning equations is: Generate 10 to 15 equations per vision or mission element. Too much detail will lose the strategic emphasis. Too little detail will prevent an in-depth understanding about what is being set forth in the element. If an element cannot be describe properly with 15 equations, then it is probably too general in nature or it involves more than one theme. It will need to be refined.*

5. Copy the final set of worksheets onto overhead transparencies before the first planning equations review session.

6. During the planning equation review session, have the authors of the planning equations review their work with the group using an overhead projector.

7. Once each equation is adjusted and agreed on by the planning team, rank preparedness for strategy first, then for structure and workforce capability. Write any pertinent notes in the far right-hand column.

8. Next rank importance. When both rankings are complete, place the appropriate number and letters in the ranking box in the preparedness/importance column. An equation can always be left pending if the group gets stuck on it. Don't worry about prioritizing now.

Up to this point in our planning process, we have worked with bits and pieces of data. It is time now to piece the data together into an incremental master plan.

7

Develop an Incremental Master Plan

Opportunity favors the prepared mind.
—Albert Einstein

M ost plans fail not because they were based on faulty content and logic, but because they were not properly organized and metered out into the organization.

After creating your planning equations, the next step in an effective transition is developing an incremental master plan. There are five stages to developing the incremental master plan: identifying

FIGURE 7.1
Step Four

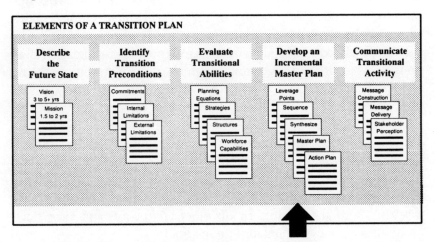

leverage points, sequencing, synthesizing, forming the master plan, and action planning.

This chapter is heavy on detail. Creating an incremental master plan is pivotal to a successful transition planning effort. In this step you will pull all the pieces of the planning effort discussed so far into a coherent, purposeful format.

Imagine an organization that consists of hundreds of cars. Each car represents an initiative, activity, project, or program. The organization's purpose is to keep the cars moving efficiently to their destinations as quickly as possible, with minimal collisions. If some of the cars become stuck in a rush-hour back up, would it help to put bigger engines in the cars? No. Redirecting some of the traffic or resequencing the way traffic enters the roadway would be better alternatives.

Organizations with no detailed incremental master plan are likely to be blind to the subtleties necessary to sequence and prioritize ongoing activities in an efficient and logical way. It is likely that they will get stuck in the trap of putting bigger engines in cars when rerouting the traffic was what was necessary. For example, the service center of a software distributor was receiving an increased number of customer complaints. Customers were upset about the apparent unavailability of service representatives to help troubleshoot problems. It was not unusual for a customer to have to wait in excess of five minutes before service was provided. The initial fix to this situation was to add capacity; more phone lines and service representatives were added. But the level of complaints did not go down as expected. Further investigation revealed that because of the specialized nature of the service conversations, many customers had to talk with multiple reps before they could find one with the right knowledge to help. This forced repeated explanations on the part of the customer, which was frustrating to them, and reduced efficiency of service personnel. Further analysis showed that because of the rapid growth of the company, and the many new and different types of software being introduced, the current rep population needed to be segmented into specialized service centers. This action increased efficiency by more than 30 percent. A new just-in-time training system for service reps was adopted and a call routing system was put in place. The end result was a substantial reduction in customer complaints and excess capacity in service personnel and phone lines.

The incremental master plan ties together all of the goals, obstacles, and resources identified in the planning process. When organizations skip this critical step, work efforts will sputter, employees will become disgruntled, performance will diminish, customers will sense that all is not well. This is the typical downward spiral of a poorly coordinated transition effort. For example, a large West Coast insurance company, in an attempt to battle declining profits and rising costs, created a new plan of attack. It included aggressive sales tactics, downsizing, systems streamlining, renegotiating hospital payment contracts, work process improvement, starting a subsidiary HMO, and employee benefits reduction. All of these tactics, identified in their transition plan, seemed appropriate and necessary. Their implementation was uncoordinated, simultaneous, and rushed. The environment was filled with turmoil and confusion. Profits did not rebound as anticipated. The board of directors elected to merge the ailing organization with a regional affiliate with a better performance track record—to large extent because they felt that poor management had allowed the organization to get out of control.

The value of the incremental master plan is fourfold:

- It documents all data and assumptions (i.e., transition preconditions, planning equations, vision/mission inputs).
- It considers all transitional activities simultaneously and judiciously, protecting resources from being squandered away across the organization.
- It provides focus, helping individuals, business units, and divisions to pull together to work toward the same goals.
- It helps the organization take one manageable, logical step at a time.

This would be a good time to assemble all of the planning materials created so far in a three-ring binder and label it "Transition Plan." This binder should include all of the data generated by the planning team and should document the logic of steps that have been undertaken.

Identifying Leverage Points

The planning team's hard work leading up to this point is about to pay off. The planning equations created in Chapter 6 can be grouped rather quickly by similar strategies. This accomplishes several things: It ensures that similar strategies will be consolidated and not be implemented independently by different functional groups with conflicting priorities. Also, the strategy groupings identify the true levers of change, the critical centers of activity that achieve the vision or mission in the most direct way. Once the leverage points are identified the organization will be able to focus available resources efficiently.

Unlike the vision or mission statement elements, which are higher-order descriptions of a future state, leverage points are groupings of detailed planning equations that identify specific areas for change in the organization. This step is many times quite revealing because it surfaces critical areas where the organization will need to focus, and these can be significantly different from where resources are currently being invested.

Our first order of business is to make sure all of the revised and ranked planning equations (reviewed on overhead transparencies) are updated on the original paper worksheets. Next, cut the planning equations apart to separate them (see Figure 7.2).

Sort the equations by like strategy—read the equations and group those that are trying to achieve the same end. Ignore the vision or mission element at the top of the equation. Our intent is to identity strategies with common purpose. Sometimes it is difficult to interpret whether the strategy of a given equation qualifies for a particular group. Added clarity may be found in the structure and workforce capability components of the equation. It is easiest to sort the equations on a large table. When you have finished, you will have groups of planning equations that look something like those in Figure 7.3.

It is possible that your planning process has generated in excess of 150 planning equations (six to ten strategic elements with ten to fifteen planning equations each). This is not an indication that the process has gone awry. There are many logical reasons for generating a lot of equations: many people on the planning team, work performed by individuals rather than in subgroups, or just a very prolific group of planners. Some clusters will have only a few equations in them, others many. The number of equations per cluster is irrelevant. There is no need to try to distribute them evenly. Each

FIGURE 7.2
Planning Equations Cut Apart

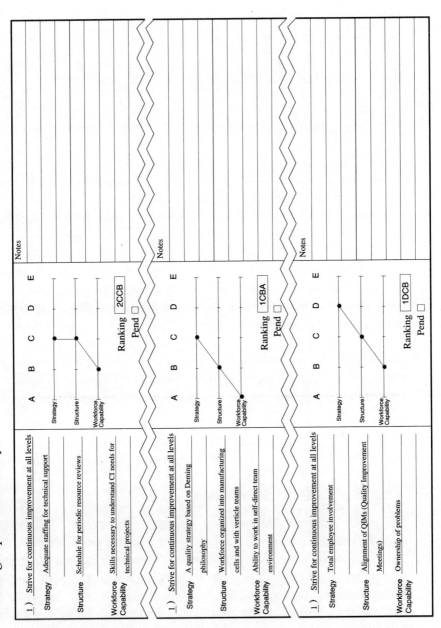

FIGURE 7.3
Forming Leverage Points

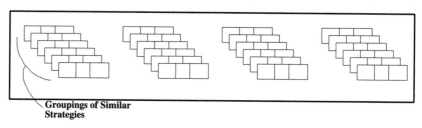

Groupings of Similar
Strategies

cluster will contain a wide mix of equations created from different vision or mission statement strategic elements.

A thorough discussion should follow the initial sorting of planning equations into leverage points. Make sure that everyone on the planning team agrees on the way the equations have been sorted.

Next, you will give a name to each leverage point. Think about the major areas of emphasis or activity the grouping suggests. The name should reflect the theme of the strategy shared by all the equations in the grouping, that is, identify a higher level strategy that encompasses all of the strategies in the grouping. If this is not possible, then the grouping needs to be resorted into different subgroupings until a clear name for each becomes apparent. Here are examples of header names used by the ACME Manufacturing Company:

- Multifunctional Work Teams
- Team-Based Culture with Appropriate Skills
- Pay and Progression System Responsive to Organization/Role Changes
- Effective Real-Time Information Systems
- Global Product Specifications

Note that the names identified are specific and descriptive in nature—Effective Real Time Information Systems tells us a lot more than simply "systems." Write the name of each leverage point above the grouping.

Once the leverage points are named, the planning team is usually amazed to see the groupings that have emerged. Some of the groupings will bear the names of initiatives or projects currently in progress; some will represent a new or different focus altogether. Most leverage points will contain a grouping of activities that has not heretofore been articulated or addressed collectively. Some leverage points may include planning equations that represent all of the vision or mission elements. Few will have equations representing only a single element. This demonstrates that the planning process is cross-functional. Here are two leverage point groupings with their associated headers identified by ACME Manufacturing:

Team-Based Culture with Appropriate Skills

5. Develop "focused factories" and use progressive work design.
   Strategy: Management commitment to flatter organization.
   Structure: Form work teams.
   WF Capability: Team work skills.

   1CCB

5. Develop "focused factories" and use progressive work design.
   Strategy: Management commitment to a flatter manufacturing organization.
   Structure: Eliminate leads.
   WF Capability: Operators w/good communication skills.

   1CBB

4. Use a team approach to continuously improve job satisfaction and productivity.
   Strategy: Encourage problem solving through teamwork.
   Structure: Reward and reinforce teamwork.
   WF Capability: Workforce skilled in team dynamics.

   1DCB

4. Use a team approach to continuously improve job satisfaction and productivity.
   Strategy: Empowerment of operators to initiate projects.
   Structure: Empowered QIMs/checkbook policy.
   WF Capability: Knowledge of how to spend money/manage projects.

   1CCB

7. Quickly respond to appropriate customer needs through adaptable manufacturing.
   Strategy: Avoid dependency on specialist operators.

    Structure: Cross-train workforce for flexibility.
WF Capability: Develop team culture.

        1BBB

5. Develop "focused factories" and use progressive work design.
    Strategy: Self-directed, high-commitment teams.
    Structure: Teams take responsibility from scheduling to delivery.
WF Capability: Training in group dynamics and team work.

        1BBB

4. Use a team approach to continuously improve job satisfaction and productivity.
    Strategy: Decision-making at grass roots.
    Structure: Proper information/performance systems.
WF Capability: Skilled, educated workforce.

        1BAB

1. Strive for continuous improvement at all levels.
    Strategy: Minimum bureaucracy for CI.
    Structure: Vertically structured, round-the-clock QIMs.
WF Capability: Intensive cross-shift communication/operators with communication skills and willingness to participate in this type of environment.

        1BDB

1. Strive for continuous improvement at all levels.
    Strategy: Multifunctional, vertical problem-solving approach.
    Structure: Product/process-focused work group structure.
WF Capability: People who work together to solve product/process problems; ability to participate in multidisciplinary team.

        1CBB

1. Strive for continuous improvement at all levels.
    Strategy: Total employee involvement.
    Structure: Focused QIMs.
WF Capability: Effective QIM leadership.

        1DCB

1. Strive for continuous improvement at all levels.
    Strategy: Total employee involvement.
    Structure: Alignment of QIMs.
WF Capability: Ownership of problems.

        1DCB

6. Be a global supplier of quality products.
    Strategy: Adaptable manufacturing.
    Structure: Team based shop floor.
    WF Capability: Team skills.

                                                      1BCB

6. Be a global supplier of quality products.
    Strategy: Adaptable manufacturing.
    Structure: Flat organization.
    WF Capability: Commitment to reduce hands-off/broader knowledge of costs, systems materials, manufacturing.

                                                      1BBB

1. Strive for continuous improvement at all levels.
    Strategy: Quality driven strategy.
    Structure: Workforce organized to allow access to change.
    WF Capability: Ability to work in a team.

                                                      1CBB

4. Use a team approach to continuously improve job satisfaction and productivity.
    Strategy: Push decision-making and accountability to grass-roots.
    Structure: Simplify decision-making process by providing information.
    WF Capability: Workforce able to analyze information for decision-making.

                                                      1BBB

Effective Real-Time Information Systems

5. Develop "focused factories" and use progressive work design.
    Strategy: Management commitment to a flatter organization.
    Structure: Accessible information systems.
    WF Capability: All operators have clear systems understanding.

                                                      1CBB

6. Be a global supplier of quality products.
    Strategy: 99% on-time delivery.
    Structure: Excellent MRP.
    WF Capability: Systems literate.

                                                      1DCB

1. Strive for continuous improvement at all levels.
   Strategy: Total Quality Management.
   Structure: Real-time systems.
   WF Capability: Data-based decision-making.

   1CAB

2. Reduce costs to enable manufacturing to meet corporate profitability targets.
   Strategy: Resources allocated to manufacturing and manufacturing support.
   Structure: Real information systems, not accounting based.
   WF Capability: Ownership of improvement at ops level—hiring criteria.

   1DBB

2. Reduce costs to enable manufacturing to meet corporate profitability targets.
   Strategy: Utilize shop floor knowledge.
   Structure: Real-time systems on the floor.
   WF Capability: Willingness to learn/knowledgeable workforce.

   1CCB

4. Use a team approach to continuously improve job satisfaction and productivity.
   Strategy: Time-based competition (decision-making cycle time).
   Structure: Flat organization.
   WF Capability: Empowered workforce/process and systems and knowledge—need structure to empower.

   1BBB

7. Quickly respond to appropriate customer needs through adaptable manufacturing.
   Strategy: Short manufacturing cycle time.
   Structure: Effective MRP system in place.
   WF Capability: Workforce with MRP skills (operators).

   1CCB

7. Quickly respond to appropriate customer needs through adaptable manufacturing.
   Strategy: Two-week turnaround on prototypes.
   Structure: Real-time systems (Databases: SMO, M.S., AMAPs, costing).
   WF Capability: WF knowledgeable in use of database.

   1BBB

2. Reduce costs to enable ACME to meet corporate profitability targets.

   Strategy: MRP based manufacturing (real time quant. system for information management).

  Structure: Regular program in maintaining and updating costs.

 WF Capability: People assigned and trained to maintain MRP.

                 1DCC

2. Reduce costs to enable manufacturing to meet corporate profitability targets.

   Strategy: Profound understanding of cause and effect.

  Structure: Develop appropriate metrics (ops. plan and monthly report).

 WF Capability: PDCA mentality.

                 1CDC

2. Reduce costs to enable manufacturing to meet corporate profitability targets.

   Strategy: Resources allocated to manufacturing and manufacturing support.

  Structure: Data readily available.

 WF Capability: Trained to interpret data.

                 1DBB

7. Quickly respond to appropriate customer needs through adaptable manufacturing.

   Strategy: Flexible manufacturing in print/cut/pack/label.

  Structure: Accessible, correct M.S. and SMO database.

 WF Capability: Workforce knowledgeable in use of SMO and M.S. databases.

                 1CBB

If the vision or mission statement elements were delegated to team members for action planning prior to generating and grouping the planning equations, two critical problems would result: Action planning would be conducted in an unintegrated (not cross-functional) fashion and the action plans would not directly address the leverage points in the organization. For example, one of the mission statement strategic elements for the ACME Manufacturing Company was "strive for continuous improvement at all levels." After sorting the planning equations into groupings and naming them, there was no leverage point with the same name as this strategic element.

The reason is that continuous improvement will involve all areas and activities in the organization. Close examination of the ACME planning equation data set reveals a wide range of continuous improvement activities imbedded in various leverage point groupings. Had continuous improvement been addressed as an isolated project, the action planning solution would not have been comprehensive enough to influence all aspects of the organization—which is a fundamental requirement of a continuous improvement program.

Before moving on to sequencing the leverage points, examine the leverage points by their importance ranking. Do any of the groupings lack at least a few equations with a number one ranking in importance? If so, highlight the grouping with a felt pen. After sequencing is performed, it will be important to note where the leverage point is located in the planning sequence. A high sequence value indicates activities that provide a foundation or enable other critically ranked activities to be performed. So, even though the grouping lacks planning equations with number one importance rankings, the grouping overall can be high in sequence. This suggests that the grouping of activities may not have received enough attention in the past because they appear to be of low priority, but are the key to achieving other critical activities. This is an example of how the complexities of business can camouflage the order in which work needs to be performed—an all-too-frequent occurrence. It is typical to find company-wide initiatives out of sequence with various divisional needs. For example, a retail company embarked on an organization-wide downsizing effort to reduce overhead. Some of the 143 retail centers were inefficient and overstaffed, others were not. This blanket initiative punished some of the well-run retail centers and rewarded the inefficient ones. Business performance plummeted. The unobvious higher sequence initiative was revamping the corporation's inefficient performance measurement system which lacked a standardized format for collecting performance data. Had this been done first, a different course of action would have certainly been taken.

Sequencing Leverage Points

With the leverage points named you are ready to put them in the order in which they will be tackled. The Interrelationship Digraph, found in Michael Brassard's *The Memory Jogger Plus+*, is an excellent tool for performing this task.

The interrelationship digraph is a simple tool used to show the driver and result relationship between two activities (also known as precursor and follower). We will use this tool to determine the sequential order of the leverage points. For example, here are two leverage point headers. Which is the driver (or precursor) and which is the result (or follower)? An arrow between the headers is used to show this relationship.

Train All Employees In New Customer Service Systems	**Identify and Install New Customer Service Systems**

In this circumstance, I would place the arrow as shown below. I would need to define the customer service system and make sure it was right for the company before investing in training employees. The arrow is drawn from the header that drives (precursor) to the header that is a result or, in this case, follows.

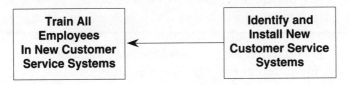

The mechanics of the digraph are straightforward. Place your leverage point headers in a circle and draw arrows to demonstrate the logical sequence between them. Start with one header and work your way around the circle asking, "What is the relationship between these two headers; which drives and which is the result? Which logically comes first?

Let's complicate the digraph by adding another leverage point header. With the addition of this new cluster header, how does the digraph change? In Figure 7.4, I have worked my way around this small circle of headers, drawing these arrows.

I felt that Develop a Customer Service Strategy was definitely the driver behind Identify and Install New Customer Service Systems. I also felt that Develop a Customer Service Strategy needed to occur

FIGURE 7.4
Sequencing Leverage Points

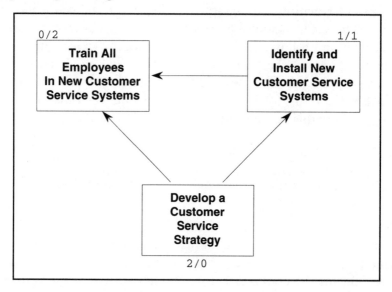

before Train All Employees In New Customer Service Systems. With the arrows drawn, the digraph is scored to determine which change point headers are the key drivers and which are simply the results of the drivers. The digraph is scored by counting the arrows that lead out (drive) and in (result) for each leverage point header.

In the upper left corner, Train All Employees in New Customer Service Systems scored a 0/2 meaning that "0" driver arrows lead out from the header and "2" arrows led in. If you look at the scoring of the three headers you will immediately see that Develop a Customer Service Strategy is the clear driver, with a score of 2/0, and Train All Employees in New Customer Service Systems, with a score of 0/2, is being driven. The interpretation of this digraph is that a customer service strategy should be developed prior to identifying and creating systems or training employees.

The interrelationship digraph really becomes invaluable with more complicated scenarios. For some headers, there will be no obvious sequential relationship with any of the others. If you cannot identify a relationship, don't draw an arrow.

Now let's look at ACME Manufacturing Company's digraph in Figure 7.5. There are thirteen leverage points. As the planning

FIGURE 7.5
ACME Manufacturing Company—Interrelationship Digraph

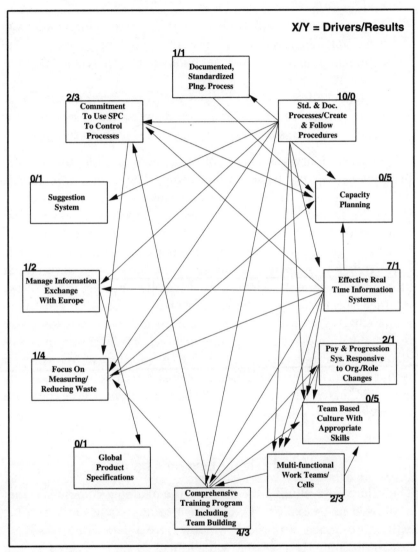

team created the digraph, they occasionally made reference to the planning equations that support the headers for clarification.

This is what they learned from the sequencing process:

1. There are three primary drivers out of the thirteen groupings on the digraph. They are, in this order, Standardize and Docu-

ment Processes 10/0; Effective Real Time Information Systems 7/1; and Comprehensive Training Program Including Team Building 4/3.

2. Many initiatives and projects that were currently underway were not key drivers. This was not apparent because of the complexity and high level of change in the current work environment.

3. A number of projects and initiatives were corporate mandates. Some of these initiatives and projects were out of sequence for the division—it was a less than optimal way to do things.

This preliminary sequencing of major activities identified in the planning process can be very enlightening. The team may learn that what they thought were top priorities must move to a lower queuing in the sequence, not because they are any less important, but simply because some other activity must be performed first to lay the proper groundwork. Also, it is likely that a number of activities deemed high in sequence in the plan are ones the organization has little or no experience performing. It can be alarming if any of the leverage points contain a large number of activities ranked "A" in preparedness (i.e., no experience; don't think we are ready to do this; many unknowns). Any grouping which has 20% or more of its planning equations ranked "A" or "B" is good cause for worry. It would be quite improbable that an organization could successfully engage in many activities in which they had little or no experience in a six- to 12-month period.

Synthesizing Leverage Points

The value of developing the detail of the planning equations is that it allowed us to explore a wide range of approaches and possible activities to reach our vision. We now have a detailed, (cross-functional) planning data set that will allow us to very quickly pick out the dominant strategies or themes in each grouping. By compiling the transition equations under each leverage point, we can identify the few critical activities or predominant strategies that can bring us closer to our goals. I call this step *synthesis*.

Synthesis is a technique for identifying one to three overarching strategies from each grouping of planning equations for each leverage point. We want to be able to answer the question, "What specific activities need to be performed in each leverage point in order to achieve the vision or mission?" We need not be concerned with actually trying to carry out all the activities represented in each planning equation. We want to extrapolate the critical few strategies and their associated structures and workforce capabilities that will offer the best return for the organization—create significant movement toward our goals.

Examine each leverage point grouping to see what key strategies emerge. Identify two or three predominant strategies that, if implemented, would achieve the desired result for that particular leverage point. The strategies that emerge from this review may be ones you already have identified in one or more of the planning equations. Other times, new strategies will emerge that are a logical blending and evolution (or synthesis) of the strategies already identified in the leverage point. This iteration of strategies—strategies grouped into leverage points, then a few predominant strategies identified for each leverage point through synthesis—helps us focus on those vital few areas that will have the greatest impact for the organization.

The planning synthesis worksheet is designed to help you complete this important activity. One worksheet should be used for each leverage point. Each leverage point should be analyzed, one at a time, in order of sequential importance.

To complete the Planning Synthesis worksheet, examine a given leverage point and:

1. Pick one to three predominant strategies. It is likely that new strategies and new equations (different ways to arrange the data) will become apparent when examining the planning equations.
2. For each, identify the logical structure and workforce capability components that will complete each new synthesis equation. Note that the new equation on the worksheet can associate up to three structures and capabilities with each strategy—because in all likelihood, it will take multiple structures and capabilities to fully achieve a given strategy.

FIGURE 7.6
Planning Synthesis Worksheet

Leverage Point: _____		
Strategy #1 _____ _____ _____	Structure #1 _____ _____ _____	Workforce Capability #1 _____ _____ _____
	Structure #2 _____ _____ _____	Workforce Capability #2 _____ _____ _____
	Structure #3 _____ _____ _____	Workforce Capability #3 _____ _____ _____
Strategy #2 _____ _____ _____	Structure #1 _____ _____ _____	Workforce Capability #1 _____ _____ _____
	Structure #2 _____ _____ _____	Workforce Capability #2 _____ _____ _____
	Structure #3 _____ _____ _____	Workforce Capability #3 _____ _____ _____
Strategy #3 _____ _____ _____	Structure #1 _____ _____ _____	Workforce Capability #1 _____ _____ _____
	Structure #2 _____ _____ _____	Workforce Capability #2 _____ _____ _____
	Structure #3 _____ _____ _____	Workforce Capability #3 _____ _____ _____

Our synthesis effort has helped us identify one to three key strategies for each leverage point. These strategies represent the pivotal activities in our transition plan. The Synthesis worksheet has also shown us the types of structure and workforce capability necessary to support the chosen direction.

Framing the Incremental Master Plan

We have gone far enough in our planning process to create a framework for the incremental master plan. To accomplish this, line up the leverage point headers in sequence based on their digraph scores. Next, assign all of the organization's activities that are in progress to the appropriate header. A quick brainstorming session will produce adequate data for this preliminary activity. Your finished product should be in the format depicted below.

A cursory examination of the groupings of activities should tell you how aligned current organizational activity is with the sequence necessary to reach your vision.

Next, add your new strategies from the Planning Synthesis worksheet. This should help complete the picture about what you have on your plate to do and in the sequence necessary to achieve it.

FIGURE 7.7
Initial Master Plan Framework

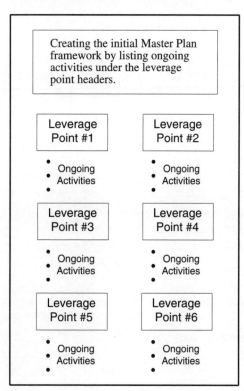

This is a good time to examine the activity mix carefully. How many of your strategies are what you might term new or where you have little experience? If the percentage of this occurrence is high, you have cause for concern. New activities take an inordinate amount of time and effort to do well. And, there is a high probability that you will not do them all well the first time. In this case, extend the time frame set for accomplishing them or lower your expectation regarding what can and will be accomplished. Don't set yourself up for failure.

Action Planning

Action Planning is the critical final step in refining the incremental master plan. The only real way to properly fine-tune transition work is to dive into the details. I would suggest, however, that the transition planning team hold off on extensive action planning until stakeholders have had a chance to review planning products generated to date. This would include the first draft of the incremental master plan. Action planning is a time-consuming activity. It doesn't make sense to commit heavily to this activity until stakeholders endorse your planning up to this point.

Actually, action planning serves many purposes that go far beyond generating detail for the planning process:

- Action planning serves as a fact-finding tool. It determines the complexity of transition activities and the organization's ability to perform them.
- Action planning provides a way for all significant players in the organization to get involved in the planning process. Action plans should not necessarily be completed by the transition planning team. On the contrary, these plans should be completed by those closest to the work—those who must ultimately perform the work. This imbeds ownership of the transition plan in the total organization.
- Action planning is an ideal way to prepare the organization for implementation. It will get everyone thinking about what is to come and the role they will play.
- Action planning is also a great refining tool for the master plan.

It forces the planners to make sure that their plan is logical and complete.

Action plans are a contract between their creators and the transition planning team. They serve as a direct link, crossing all boundaries, divisions, and political empires, from the transition planners to those actually performing the work. Action plans should also give some indication of:

• time and resource requirements
• the short-term value (increased profits, cost savings, etc.)
• the long-term value (increased profits, cost savings, etc.)

One final advantage of extensive action planning has to do with documentation. Frequently, organizations will engage in activities for reasons that are forgotten a week or month later. If planning activity is to be taken seriously and to genuinely provide a benefit, certain controls must be in place to ensure compliance. Action plans, developed and signed by the doers and governed by the transition planning team, have teeth. They document the logic behind how a particular activity can be done, its benefit to the organization and its associated resource requirements. They are directly linked to the organization's overall plan.

An advantage of documentation has to do with organizational learning. When something doesn't go well, the action plan can be examined, and the logic behind the approach taken can be adjusted accordingly to prevent the organization from committing the same mistake again and again and again.

To complete action plans, assign the strategies in the master plan to the team leaders or individual contributors responsible for their implementation. Have them review their strategy and its associated structures and workforce capabilities. If an action planning team feels that the structure and workforce capability requirements associated with a particular strategy are not appropriate, then it is incumbent on them to share their reasoning with the planning team. If structural and capability outcomes are proposed that differ from what the planners originally intended, the overall design of the transition plan may be altered. The organization needs to know this prior to deploying resources in pursuit of their overall goals. Make

FIGURE 7.8
Action Plan

Prepared by:	Date:	Division:	Department:

Planning Activity Name:
\# _____

Strategy _____
Structure _____
Workforce Capability _____

What is the purpose of the Action Plan:

No.	Tasks	What steps would you take to accomplish this task?	Who is responsible?	What is the due date?	How will you know if this task has been completed correctly?

adjustments as necessary. If the action planning team agrees with the earlier work, they should complete the action planning form by outlining the key tasks or milestones necessary and the smaller tasks to accomplish the strategy. Have the project leader or individual contributor name a person accountable or associated with each task (in some cases each step), estimate a completion date and how success will be measured.

Here is one example of an action planning format. Note that a "metric" or measure should accompany each listed task. This tends to force the action planner into result/benefit thinking, reducing the number of low-value or no-value tasks. If the work is cross-functional and involves many people or departments, the project leader should be carefully chosen (influence skills necessary) and political/official positioning be given careful consideration.

Action plans should be completed by those closest to the work, outside of the planning environment. This serves as an additional check and balance for the efficacy of the plan. Note that at the top of the action plan there is a space to list strategy, structure and workforce capability. This helps ensure that those chartered with action planning will follow the original intent of the transition planners.

After experiencing the planning process to this point, a bank's district manager applied the concepts learned during the action planning phase. He assigned an action plan to his eighteen branch managers. The strategy: transition to a sales culture. The structure: create a procedure to increase the frequency of sales opportunities with customers. The workforce capability: improve the ability of sales representatives (platform officers) to make contact with and discuss the bank's products with customers. The action planning team came up with a very effective sequence of steps to assist their administratively oriented employees in their transition to a sales culture. The planning equations showed that the bank's branch offices lacked the necessary structure to facilitate sales contacts and workforce capability showed that the basic sales skills were lacking. During action planning, the team came up with a unique solution. They developed the 15, 10, 2 rule. The branch sales employees were required to make 15 telephone calls per week to current customers to check on their level of satisfaction and see if there was anything they could do to help. Just a quick status check. Ten times a week, sales employees were required to get up from their desks and introduce themselves to a customer walking through the branch, someone they currently did not know. Finally, twice each week, each sales employee was required to leave the branch and visit two merchants that were not currently doing business with the bank. The branch managers had also created reporting forms to ensure that this mandate was followed.

This may not sound too dramatic. That was really the brilliance of the system. The action planning team had introduced a series of new activities which required a high degree of sales behavior not normally seen in employees. They had also created a incremental system which had made it relatively easy for the employees' supervisors to follow up each day. In this way, if someone was not performing the required tasks, a supervisor could easily coach them in time to make his quota, long before the end of the week arrived. Some employees found this type of activity so distasteful that they either left the bank or transferred to other jobs. But this was a very small percentage. Most employees actually began to enjoy the new activity. As they became comfortable with the increased levels of interaction with customers, the branch managers began modifying the requirements. Gradually, over time, they had administratively based staff performing routines which would be more closely associated with sales people. The overall behavior change was significant. This incremental method of installing the new routine was acceptable to most of the employees.

When I describe this scenario to managers, they sometimes say to me, "You're spoon-feeding them. Tell them what you expect. If they can't perform the tasks, get someone who can. We don't have time to baby-sit or nursemaid employees when we're paying them good money." In some cases I might agree with this. But those cases are relatively few and restricted to circumstances where an organization will be out of business tomorrow if they don't have the right people performing the right jobs immediately. When the requirements of the job change so radically that the needed behavior change from employees requires them to transform into a completely different personality type or occupational focus you might not be able to use this incremental approach. But most of the time, the changes required are either not too significant, or if significant, can be shaped over a period of years. In this case, a detailed incremental plan will create the least amount of carnage and the least disturbance to your customer base, and will shift workforce capability in pace with new organizational strategies and structures. This is a good example of linking what has been identified in planning equations to the action planning phase.

With action planning complete, the incremental master plan can be completed. Action planning generates a level of detail that allows for the scheduling of activities by quarter (shorter or longer time frames may be appropriate for your organization). Figure 7.9 is an example of ACME Manufacturing's completed incremental master plan. A number of activities have been redistributed to focus on the leverage points, which are the top three headers listed on the plan.

Once we have assembled the incremental master plan (fully loaded in this form), we now are in a position to make a sound judgment regarding new activities and initiatives not included in the plan. It is not always possible or easy to reorder activities that are already in process—but sometimes it is necessary. If a new initiative has merit—if a context now exists to evaluate it—a case can be made to either queue it up or drop it.

As a final step, resource requirements can be added to the incremental master plan, which include: cost, time, person days. I call this step *resource loading*. The people time needed to complete projects, the project days, project calendar days (a 20-day project could take four calendar months to complete), and available resources indicate how fast you can proceed. This can be a powerful tool for negotiating additional resources or changing due dates on previous work commitments.

At this point, it should become clear whether or not the organization's resources are being allocated in alignment with its transitional objectives. Activities should be focused around the key strategies identified on the planning synthesis worksheets and against those leverage points that are considered the key drivers.

The incremental master plan can be refined over time by creating action plans for all of the activities in the queue. Action planning will generate very specific information around timing, resources, and the types of tasks you need to perform.

The key goal of the transition planning effort is to produce an understandable planning document that clearly communicates the

FIGURE 7.9
Master Plan with Schedule of Activities

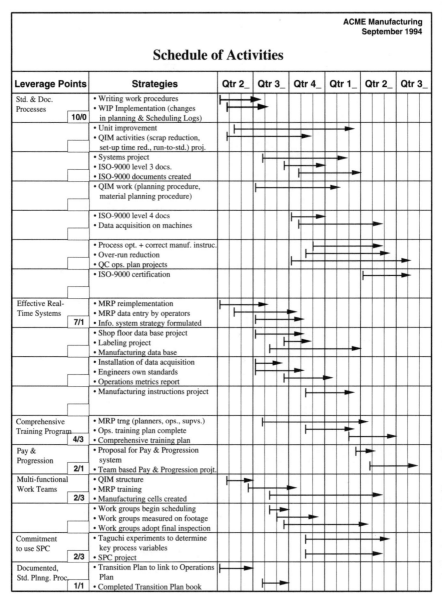

ACME Manufacturing
September 1994

Schedule of Activities

Leverage Points	Strategies	Qtr 2_	Qtr 3_	Qtr 4_	Qtr 1_	Qtr 2_	Qtr 3_
Std. & Doc. Processes **10/0**	• Writing work procedures • WIP Implementation (changes in planning & Scheduling Logs)						
	• Unit improvement • QIM activities (scrap reduction, set-up time red., run-to-std.) proj.						
	• Systems project • ISO-9000 level 3 docs. • ISO-9000 documents created						
	• QIM work (planning procedure, material planning procedure)						
	• ISO-9000 level 4 docs • Data acquisition on machines						
	• Process opt. + correct manuf. instruc. • Over-run reduction • QC ops. plan projects						
	• ISO-9000 certification						
Effective Real-Time Systems **7/1**	• MRP reimplementation • MRP data entry by operators • Info. system strategy formulated						
	• Shop floor data base project • Labeling project • Manufacturing data base						
	• Installation of data acquisition • Engineers own standards • Operations metrics report						
	• Manufacturing instructions project						
Comprehensive Training Program **4/3**	• MRP trng (planners, ops., supvs.) • Ops. training plan complete • Comprehensive training plan						
Pay & Progression **2/1**	• Proposal for Pay & Progression system • Team based Pay & Progression projt.						
Multi-functional Work Teams **2/3**	• QIM structure • MRP training • Manufacturing cells created						
	• Work groups begin scheduling • Work groups measured on footage • Work groups adopt final inspection						
Commitment to use SPC **2/3**	• Taguchi experiments to determine key process variables • SPC project						
Documented, Std. Plnng. Proc. **1/1**	• Transition Plan to link to Operations Plan • Completed Transition Plan book						

logic on which it is based, the activities prescribed and the way they will be managed.

Our transition planning effort is coming to an end. But there are a few activities we must perform to complete the plan. The next chapter explores how to communicate our transition planning effort to the organization as deployment begins.

Summary Steps

There are five steps to creating an incremental master plan: identifying leverage points, sequencing, synthesizing, forming the master plan, and action planning.

Identifying Leverage Points

1. Planning equation ranking and wordsmithing done on transparencies should be transferred back to the original paper worksheets.
2. Cut the worksheets apart.
3. Using a large table surface, have the planning team group the equations by like strategy. If any confusion exists as to the nature of a particular strategy (what its true intent is), look to the structural and workforce capability components for clarification. Note: Do not group by like vision or mission element. This will defeat the value of this step by preventing cross-functional strategies from being grouped together.
4. Once the sorting has been completed the planning team should review and reach consensus on each cluster.
5. Name each grouping of planning equations. The group name or header should express action. Instead of "system" as the header, "Create Effective Real-Time Systems" more appropriately describes the nature of the collective strategies in the group. If a grouping is difficult to name, resort it.

Sequencing Leverage Points

1. Create an interrelationship digraph by placing the leverage point headers in a circle on an easel. Arrange the headers so that they are evenly spaced and allow room for arrows to connect the boxes through the center.

2. Choose a starting point. Ask the question: "Does this drive or result from the next header in the circle?" Alternative phrasing is: "Is this leverage point a precursor or follower of the next?" Draw a connecting arrow between the headers from the driver or precursor. If no relationship can be seen, do not draw an arrow. Continue to repeat this step until the relationship between all headers has been determined.

3. Score the digraph by counting outgoing and incoming arrows for each header. A header with three arrows going out and six coming in would be scored as 3/6. Three is the driver score and six is the result score. (This grouping of strategies will not rank high in the digraph sequence.) Save the digraph for later transcription and inclusion in the transition planning job book.

Synthesizing Leverage Points

1. Examine each grouping.
2. Pick the predominant two or three strategies (new strategies may become apparent when examining the planning equations) that best represent this collection of equations.
3. For each synthesis strategy, identify the logical structure and workforce capability components that will be necessary to achieve it. It is acceptable to list up to three structures and workforce capabilities for each synthesized strategy.

Forming the Incremental Master Plan

1. Create a new set of identical leverage point headers. Arrange these in a vertical column. Have the planning team brainstorm a project, initiative, and program list of ongoing activities for each header. This will serve to create the initial framework for a master plan and will eventually evolve when detailed action planning output is included.
2. Examine the Planning Synthesis worksheets. Include the new projects, initiatives and programs in the master plan.

This is a good time for the planning team to step back from the process and discuss what has been learned. Are current resources being allocated appropriately? Does the plan call for many new activities which the organization is unprepared to do?

Action Planning

The transition planning team should not, whenever possible, bear responsibility for completing action plans. This is an important opportunity to engage others in the planning process. This responsibility should be owned by individuals and teams closest to the work being addressed.

1. Complete the identification boxes on the form. List the planning activity name and number. This information will be found on the Planning Synthesis worksheet under consideration.
2. List the key strategy, structures, and workforce capabilities that support this activity, found on the Planning Synthesis worksheet.
3. Brainstorm the various tasks that would need to be completed to achieve this activity. There is no limit to the number of tasks. Use as many worksheets as required.
4. Rank the tasks in the order that they need to be performed. Number them on the Action Plan.
5. Further define each task. List the steps necessary to accomplish each task.
6. The action planning team should try to reach consensus on the work to be performed including all the detailed steps, and then assign the tasks. It is possible that someone assigned a task will not be present during action planning. If this is the case, it is usually best to review the Action Plan with these individuals prior to announcing assignments.
7. Due dates should be negotiated with the action planning team and all responsible parties. Greatest clarity and commitment is achieved when all participants fully understand their role in the overall plan.
8. Identify measures, metrics, or milestones for all of the tasks. Ask the question: "How will the action planning team know if the tasks are on track and proceeding as planned?"

With action plans complete, integrate this information into the master plan and create a master schedule if desired.

Action plans are a key, short-term method for ensuring expected results for the overall transition plan. This activity is a critical implementation vehicle and should be given proper time and attention.

Additionally, resource commitments for all of the new projects and activities identified in the planning process will need to be estimated. Guesstimating these requirements will do fine for all known activities. First-cut action planning should be created for unknown projects and initiatives prior to estimating requirements. This will help generate realistic numbers.

When action planning a strategy that is new to the organization (little or no experience doing this task) benchmarking may be an appropriate interim step. This will help estimate the true resource commitments necessary to achieve the task.

8

Communicate
Transitional Activity

Unhappy is a people that has run out of words to describe what is going on.
—Thurman Arnold

Some would argue that communicating in large organizations tends to be a convoluted activity even at the best of times. Add to this the problems of distortion that arise during transition and one might think there is little chance of offering precise, clear communications during an organizational transition. This is probably a fairly safe assumption. It means that extra care must go into design-

FIGURE 8.1
Step Five

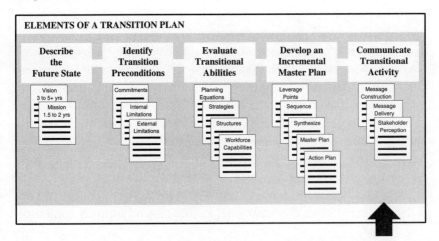

ing a communication plan. Nothing will derail effective transition faster than ineffective communication. It is essential to seek, and often influence opinions of management, peers, employees, and customers about your transition effort. The opinions of your stakeholders will greatly influence your ultimate ability to carry out your transition plan; if they are not supportive, you may be faced with a difficult, up-hill effort.

Even though it is represented as the last of five steps in this planning model, communication needs to begin up front in the transition process. The first communication about transition tends to be shy on content since it isn't developed yet, but it can be rich on context—which explains the process and how employees will be involved.

Communication is so vital to the ultimate success of your transition plan that a mediocre transition plan communicated well will probably help contribute to smooth organizational change; a brilliant transition plan poorly communicated will undoubtedly fail. A transition plan that does not treat communication methodology in a formalized way is incomplete and exposes the organization to risk. The following vignette illustrates what can happen to a well-planned but poorly communicated transition.

While working for a large consulting firm, I received an assignment to replace a consultant on a troubled account. My colleague had been working with the account, a large east coast retailer, for about six months. Progress to date included a rather straightforward transition plan. Implementation of the plan was to begin with closure and consolidation of several stores, a renewed emphasis on customer service, especially at the point of sale, and an increase of local store control through decentralized buying. Only 5 percent of the total workforce (which numbered above eight thousand) faced any real possibility of job loss, and people willing to relocate were guaranteed continued employment. This was not a radical transition by any stretch of the imagination. And yet, six months into it, sales had dipped 22 percent (not related to the position of that industry at the time), customer complaints and unsolicited employee turnover were mounting, and worst of all, local newspapers were indicting management for mishandling the reorganization.

What had gone wrong? The same thing that derails many organizations during critical transitional periods—problems in communication. Management simply was not keeping employees informed. It perceived the transition as proceeding as planned. The only communication reaching employees was information communicated out of context through the employee grapevine. As an outsider uninvolved in the development and initial implementation of the plan, it was easy to see where the organization's workforce, responding to rumor, their worst fears, and a lack of reliable information, had developed mass anxiety. The transition plan had been constructed by the executive group and the consultant behind closed doors.

The first problem began when the planning team needed to gather data from employees. Information began to leak out, including a rumor about significant store closures and staff cuts. Employees hearing this rumor did not have the benefit of knowing the overall context of the transition plan. Even after management became aware that these rumors were traveling through the organization's grapevine, they did nothing to quell them. Employees had little concrete information to offset their active imaginations. It didn't take long before employees had conjured up a number of worst-case scenarios, and actually began believing them.

By the time the transition plan was announced, employees were in such a frenzy that any communication was difficult for them to absorb, let alone something as complex as the details of a transition. At best, bits and pieces of information got through. Management no longer had much credibility. Employees didn't believe the communications they heard. Some of the initial transition activities, even though very limited in nature, were poorly timed and further convinced employees that their misperceptions must be correct. For example, one of the first transition actions was to close a store, displacing 50 employees. Although no other store closures were planned, this one fueled the employee perception that more closures were on the way. Management must have been lying to them.

I learned from this experience that communication during transition cannot be left to chance. Communications should be considered in a systematic way, concurrent with each step along the planning journey.

We did manage to fix this communication crisis using a simple, four-step solution. Step 1 was to create a video explaining the complete story. This was shown at each store, with a core group of executives present to answer questions following the video. When the executive group left, a second question and answer period was conducted with local management. Second, the incremental steps of the transition plan were posted where all employees could see them. The posters included dates, actions, and timelines. This total disclosure took the mystery out of the transition process for employees. Third, each business unit discussed each of the transition steps, its possible impact and what they would need to do to manage their own part of the transition. Each business unit submitted a plan for supporting the transition. All stores reviewed each other's inputs and were asked to evaluate the plan and submit feedback. An addendum was added to the plan to show the specifics of any planned layoffs, including dates, locations, and other pertinent information. Employees affected by layoffs were given opportunities to relocate, job training in preparation for other positions or a chance to take early retirement. They received such excellent treatment that other employees thought them lucky. This approach put fears of job security to rest and insured employee buy-in and focus even in this chaotic transitioning environment. Finally, a transition newsletter was distributed weekly to provide detailed information about the status of the transition. This was supplemented by periodic videos and visits from the senior management group. Each newsletter also included a suggested activity for business units to conduct during their weekly team meetings to help employees learn about and understand the dynamics of the transition. All communications were intended to be two-way; employees were expected to give input to the transition planning team, who responded in writing to all input received.

Communication is especially important, and especially difficult, during times of transition. A transitional communication plan should be given careful attention, as it is the primary vehicle for implementing the tasks set forth in the transition plan. In developing a communication plan, you will need to think about three challenges:

1. structuring messages to communicate what you want
2. delivering messages
3. managing stakeholder perception

Structuring Messages to Communicate What You Want

There are three primary ways in which adults learn: visually/experientially (we see someone do it, model it or show it, or we actually experience doing it ourselves), through written information (we read books or view overhead slides with information written on them), and conceptually (through the spoken word supplemented with examples, graphics, metaphors, and analogies).

Some individuals are more receptive to certain learning methods than others and people in certain occupations tend to have similar learning orientations. For example, attorneys characteristically are skilled at learning from written text. Academicians are noted for their aptitude for conceptual learning. An individual that works in a factory doing a repetitive task is likely to learn from watching and repeating. This doesn't mean that factory workers can't learn through reading and conceptualization or that some individuals in these jobs will not have differing learning styles and preferences, but it does mean that they are likely to be less practiced in other learning methods. If you want to communicate effectively with them, you will be most successful if you use the learning style they are most comfortable with and most practiced in using.

If your target audience consists of a mixture of occupational types with different learning propensities or if you simply don't know the audience mix, you had better be sure that your message is communicated through all three learning channels. This will guarantee the highest level of absorption. If, however, you know the learning propensities of your audience, use that knowledge to design a communication that they are likely to understand. With factory workers, make every effort to structure key messages in a visual/experiential format. Of course, this is easier said than done. Managers tend to become limited to conceptual/written communication methods. I once asked a CEO to be sure his presentation was as visual as possible. He came to the meeting and presented 20 overhead transparencies of written material. When I confronted him after the presentation, he replied, "What do you mean? I used at least 20 visuals to make my point!"

Using what we know about how adults learn and the ways they best receive information, we can understand why and where communication processes begin to break down. When the CEO of a company stands up in front of the employees and describes his vision of the future organization, chances are he is talking in a conceptual style. And—you guessed it—most employees of the average organization will receive information best through visual/experiential communication. What the CEO thinks he is communicating and what the employees are hearing are two very different things. During transition, just when it is most critical for communication to be clear and accurate, the reverse tends to happen. The CEO scratches his head and says, "I can't say it any clearer than that!" Employees scratch their heads and say, "We just heard from the top guy and we don't think he even knows what he is talking about." This is the point at which the best transition plan goes down the drain.

The model in Figure 8.2 is used to explain how communication can become disrupted in an organization. Although this model oversimplifies and generalizes learning and motivation theories, it is useful in describing the many ways communication runs amok in organizations. This graphic helps demonstrate that employees situated toward the top of the organizational hierarchy (management and senior staff) tend to:

- be self-directed
- have the ability (or need) to work in abstract, less structured environments
- think in terms of the future (at least from a quarterly view)
- be motivated by fulfilling social or higher level needs, and
- be practiced written and conceptual learners.

Employees located at the lower end of the organization hierarchy (probably 70 percent of the workforce) tend to:

- work in directed environments (they have been historically told what to do)
- have a finite work orientation (they are not comfortable dealing with abstract situations)
- have immediate, short-term orientations
- be motivated by physiological, safety or social needs (socioeconomic considerations)
- tend to be visual and experiential, not written and conceptual, learners.

FIGURE 8.2
Factors That Affect Communication

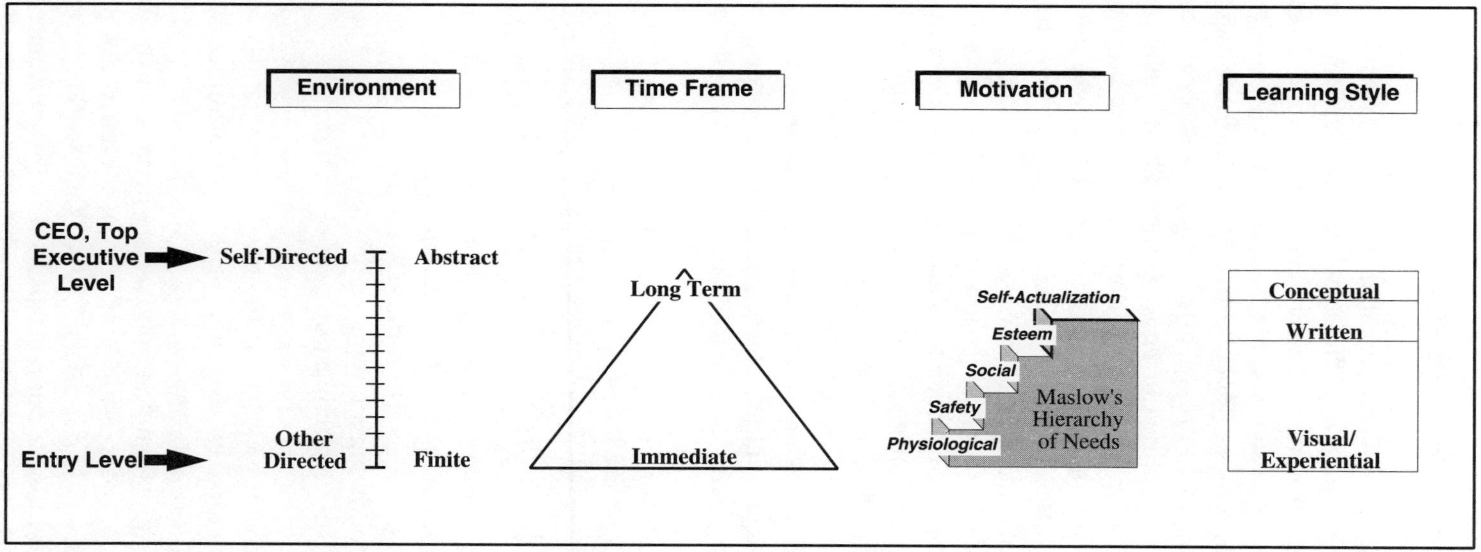

Where people are situated in the organization and why they work there greatly influences how they act and react to what is going on around them. The further up in the organization you move, the greater the probability you will find an environment where employees think, motivate, and learn on a more conceptual, abstract, and future-oriented level. And here lies the root problem in communicating during transition: These highly conceptual individuals typically are charged with the task of creating the messages to be communicated to the employee body, which is likely to prefer a very different communication style. Unless the individual or group of individuals creating these messages is well acquainted with the communication style of the workforce at large, most messages, though intended for the entire organization, will reach only a minority of employees—those at the management level and others who happen to respond well to this style.

What does this tell us? It tells us to keep our communications targeted at the largest common denominator in the organization—the average employee. It tells us not to use abstract terms. It tells us to create a communication plan that transmits the message to all employees. It tells us to be careful about how we institute change. If we have something to communicate, we must find a way to say it in simple, finite terms.

On a positive note, workforce skills and knowledge have been increasing. Team and quality initiatives, general manufacturing, and service demands have all required sophistication of the average employee—improving their ability to assimilate abstract, written, and conceptual messages. The communication gap still exists, however, and it is better to err on the side of message over-simplification.

The following are some guidelines to follow when you construct any type of communication plan or system:

- Make the message clear—use language and vocabulary that is understood by everyone in the organization. With few exceptions, written communication should not exceed an eighth-grade reading level unless you have evidence that the average employee's comprehension is at a higher level. For instance, the word "mission" is not a term the average worker typically can relate to. So mission can be translated to "what we are going to go do over the next one to two years." A conceptual term like "matrix organization" may not be translatable. So don't use it. Don't rely on people further down in the organization to translate or convert communications to make them more understandable.

- Use plenty of repetition—deliver the message enough times to penetrate the noise generated by a transitioning organization. A good rule of thumb is to repeat every message at least twice.
- There should be a high degree of message consistency—messages should be linked to what has been communicated before and what will come after. Everyone should be able to see the correlation.
- The communication should be delivered through multiple channels—recognizing that different people send and receive information on different levels, communications should be distributed systematically using a wide variety of communication styles, through different media (audio, written, video, meetings, one-on-one), hitting all three learning styles.
- Mechanisms are in place to test for understanding immediately after the message is sent—surveys, sampling, phone polls, meeting debriefs, and informal interviews are conducted regularly and following each critical communication.
- Commitments (communication dates, transition milestones) are kept unless advance notice is given that they cannot be, hopefully with a good explanation.
- The communication plan is formally owned and managed as part of the transition plan—the responsibility for communications is not delegated away from the individual or group managing the transition plan.
- The frequency of communications is formalized—employees know when to expect new information and how they will receive it.

Delivering Messages

The communication plan is a key component of the transition planning process. It is a tangible document; a subsection of the transition plan. How do you know your communication plan will be effective? An effective plan will be directly linked to the timing and sequencing of the various stages and major milestones of the transition plan. For example, communication milestones might look like this:

1. Communicate that a transition planning process has begun. The significant milestones include: research, creating or refining a vision statement, planning meetings, creating a master plan, action planning that will involve all departments and people, many opportunities for employees to have input and participate on a variety of levels, the general time line, and when to expect the next communiqué.
2. Communicate what was learned from the research phase and get input about data content and what it means, for example, an employee survey might be used in the research phase. The results should be shared and feedback solicited from those surveyed.
3. Communicate the draft vision or mission statement and get feedback to refine the document.
4. Communicate the draft master plan and get feedback to refine the document.
5. Communicate the action planning process and specific data to affected units about action planning results.
6. Communicate the refined master plan and upcoming deployment steps.
7. As the plan changes with time, keep the organization informed of those developments.

Transitions tend to distort or even destroy an organization's normal communication patterns. A certain degree of distortion should be considered normal given the pressures of change. Employees' confusion, fear, and anger impede their ability to objectively receive and comprehend information. Distorted communications bombard the organization with a continuous series of shock waves, something like what happens when you drop rocks into a stillwater pond. At some point, the pond becomes so choppy that it is difficult to separate a single wave pattern from the collective effect. Likewise, in organizations it is difficult to identify any single piece of information as reliable. Employees and managers no longer know what to believe. Not everyone hears the same story. This results in many radically different interpretations of the same message, all based on incomplete information.

The company "rumor mill" or "grapevine" is a major source of message distortion. Let's say you have a nucleus of people working on planning the organization's transition strategy and they agree, "What we discuss must stay in this room." Those individuals must perform a variety of tasks, such as collecting data from and discussing action items with others. They wind up revealing some or all of the so-called confidential planning information to people they rely on for more detailed data. These employees, who were not part of the planning team, now have access to incomplete and unfinished planning information. However, they are not bound by the same agreement to keep things quiet. Nor do they fully understand the context of the information they hold. In order for this new group of employees to fulfill the data collection requirements requested of them, they, in turn, involve yet another, broader circle of employees who are yet another step further from the planning nucleus. Before you know it, premature, incomplete, and sometimes confidential information works its way into the mainstream of the organization. It doesn't take long for the rumor mill to evolve this piecemeal information into a series of highly distorted messages, based on incomplete information. This process inevitably generates a series of misinterpretations that can fuel employee confusion, fear, and anger. By the time senior management finalizes and attempts to communicate the planning process, the distorted messages already have been hashed over 1,000 times by the workforce. Morale and productivity have already suffered, and the workforce will remain unreceptive to the intended transition scenario until the misconceptions have first been cleared away.

Other groups also leak information into the work environment, often more quickly than the rumor mill. These include support departments, such as human resources, finance, strategic planning, quality, and MIS. These groups are outside the inner circle of senior management, but they work with senior management to help create and implement key undertakings. These groups are privy to information at a very high level—information that is not completely thought through and not ready for general distribution. Without any bad intention, these groups disseminate huge amounts of information into the workplace.

As the saying goes, information is power. People feel powerful when they have access to information other people don't have. And there is a tendency to want to display this power by showing off the information to others. The very act of sharing privileged information seems to give the sender a sense of importance: "I have access to inner-circle information you don't have!"

How do you stop premature information from leaking out into the organization and derailing your planning process? You can't. But what you can do is reduce the potency of the information that leaks by providing a context for it. Once you plan your transition activities, announce them. Glut the communication channels with the messages you want to be heard. Let employees know what is going on, what to expect, when to expect it, and how any adverse or difficult situations will be handled (such as employee layoffs, reorganizations, etc.). Take the mystery out of the process. Let employees know how and when their input will be solicited and used. Above all else, never make the organization guess what is going on. Most people will guess the worst. Prevent rumors by sharing the facts.

Emphasize the importance of not disclosing undigested information to all involved in the planning process. You can't stop the grapevine, but you can beat it at its own game. If it sounds like you will have to make a major investment in communications, you are right. It is well worth the effort. Prichett & Associates (a Dallas, Texas, research and consulting firm) suggests that, on average, worker productivity reduces to 45 percent during unstable, transitional periods. This is caused by employee anxiety and general disruption in the environment, much of which can be alleviated by direct communication.

Managing Stakeholder Perception

I can recount many instances where teams faced with change plan a transition but never get the chance to carry it out. Why? Because the stakeholders, those with a vested interest in the success of the plan, don't believe the team will be successful in implementing it. This stakeholder group usually consists of high-level managers, peer managers, employees, customers, vendors, and high-level support personnel from various functional areas of the organization. If members of the stakeholder group have problems with the way the transition is being planned and managed, consider it a serious problem. Not all of the stakeholder groups directly influence your success or failure, but their indirect influence can be just as powerful.

Employees are one group that exercises powerful, indirect influence. Employees serve as a barometer for measuring how things are going. Other stakeholder groups will undoubtedly use them to test the effectiveness of your transition effort. Don't be so naive as to believe that just because they work for you they will support your plan. If they do not feel that the transition effort is in the employees' best interest, and you haven't clearly answered the all-important question, "What's in it for them?" you will face a serious transitional block. All stakeholder groups influence each other, and all have considerable influence over your success.

Many studies have been conducted on the role of stakeholder perception. Adamson Research Institute found no correlation between product quality and market share after studying 210 medium- to large-size corporations, looking at the relation between buyer motivation and product quality. The research concluded that there is a direct correlation, however, between perception of product quality and market share. The company that is best at selling the perception that they have the best product, owns the corresponding market share. This is not to say that product quality isn't also important. In order to be competitive, a product must have an acceptable degree of quality relative to the competition. But we must not only be competent at creating and delivering a product or service, we must be equally competent in communicating the perception (to our stakeholders) that we are competent at what we are doing.

When I discuss perception management I tend to get some resistance, even disbelief, that perception can play such a powerful role. Some individuals get irritated. "You're saying it is not enough to be good at my job. Now I have to become some kind of politician." True. If you are not on top of and actively managing stakeholder perception, you are not in control. After completing the first five steps of the planning process, the transition team should be pretty well equipped to identify stakeholder perceptions and manage them. Figure 8.3 lists five questions you can use to identify and manage stakeholder perception.

Figure 8.4 is an example of how ACME Manufacturing applied this model in creating their communication plan.

Each group was identified as completely as possible, including the names of specific individuals when possible. Next, the planning team answered the question, "What perception do you want each

FIGURE 8.3

Managing Stakeholder Perception

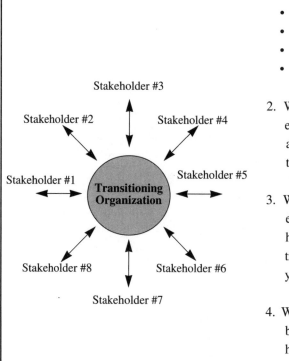

1. Who are the stakeholders?
   (individuals and groups)
   - management
   - peers
   - employee groups
   - other divisions
   - shareholders
   - suppliers
   - customers
   - board of directors

2. What perception do you want
   each stakeholder group to have
   and to convey about your transition?

3. What perception do you think
   each stakeholder group already
   holds about your organiza-
   tion/transition activities? How do
   you know?

4. What specific information must
   be communicated to each stakeholder group in order to form the
   desired perception?

5. How will you know if your communication strategy is successful?

FIGURE 8.4
ACME Manufacturing Stakeholder Groups

1. Management
   • upper managers and support function auditors
2. Peer Groups
   • peer managers inside and outside of the division
3. Employee Groups
   • supervisors, leads, operators, engineers, administrative, technicians, logistics and maintenance
4. External
   • sales force
5. Customers
   • direct and distributors

stakeholder group to have and to convey about your transition?" The team identified eight perception points where stakeholders had expressed interest or concern. They used these points (illustrated in Figure 8.5) as the basis of their perception management activity.

Next the planning team tried to describe in detail the perception each stakeholder group probably held about their organization. As

FIGURE 8.5
Perception Management Focal Points

1—The management team is in control
2—The management team has a transition plan
3—The team is executing the plan competently
4—The team is achieving its transitional goals
5—The team will not be diverted from its course of action
6—The transition plan is consistent with company goals and in support of other teams
7—The plan has benefits for the company

they began to corroborate information, it became clear some gaps existed and that it would be helpful to get further verification from the stakeholders themselves. The types of questions and concerns voiced by various stakeholders led the planning team to believe that there already were some stakeholder perception problems. For instance, meetings with several stakeholders revealed concerns about whether a clear direction had been determined and if management was in control of the situation.

Finally, the ACME Manufacturing team made a determination of the specific information to be communicated back to each stakeholder group to reinforce or correct perceptions. In particular, they felt that management would be most interested in items 1 through 5 of the perception points; peer groups, item 6; external, 7; and customers, 1 through 5 and 7. Next they crafted an outline for how to approach and verify the perceptions held by each stakeholder group. They found that the stakeholders themselves were the best at identifying the answer to how they would gauge satisfaction with and success of their particular business.

Communications cannot be left to chance. A manager once said to me, "You know, when we talked about creating a communication plan, I thought it was a real good idea. But I didn't understand the importance of it. The other day, I found myself invited to an informal meeting with senior managers to give them a progress report on transitioning our manufacturing facility. This informal gathering turned into an inquisition of sorts. The questions were pointed, almost accusatory. Although I don't think it was the intention of these senior managers to put me on the spot, in many ways I was. I found myself becoming defensive, even emotional. They had the facts all wrong. But they were obviously information poor; at least they did not have the right information. It was a lose-lose situation. In retrospect, had I been more proactive in managing their perceptions, I would never have wound up in this situation. The question that keeps nagging at me is, will I ever get a chance to finish the work I've started or will I get reorganized out of the organization or to a penalty box in some less vital part of the company. I guess I own the outcome, whichever way it turns out. The perception was always there for me to manage. It just never occurred to me to make it part of my job."

Summary Steps

- After assembling the right team for your transition planning activity, outline the communication plan. This should include: the overall framework for the transition planning process, major milestones or products, how employees will be involved and at what levels, the frequency of communiqués, and the overall timeline.
- Before proceeding with the planning process, communicate your transition process.
- Identify key stakeholders, which can be individuals or groups.
- Answer the five questions regarding stakeholder perception for each of the stakeholder groups.
- Use the communication framework as a way to refine and check your planning activity at its various stages, and as the deployment vehicle when it is time to move to implementation.

9

When and Where to Get Help

When the fox preaches, look to your geese.
—German Proverb

It is possible that you will need help at some point during your organization's transition. This chapter will help you determine whether you need help and find out what kinds of help are available both internally and externally. Finally, you will learn some valuable tips to help you assemble your transition management team.

How to Determine Whether You Need Help

If you have read this book page for page from the beginning, you should be able to assess your own preparedness to create a transition plan. Consider the makeup and competence of the transition planning team. Do you have the right mix of knowledge and experience? How comfortable do you and the leader of the planning effort feel about the task at hand? How did you do on the "Assembling the Right Team" test in Chapter 3? If you are uncertain about your organization's level of readiness, help may be in order.

What if you feel intimidated by the whole concept of organizational transition? As a leader, you will probably be hesitant to display self-doubt. Should you throw up your hands and call the nearest consulting group? No! In fact, you have a lot of work to do before you should let someone from the outside come in and confuse things further. Your first task is to learn what it is you don't know, that is, you need to begin the planning process by following the transition

147

planning steps at least through the creation of a vision statement. At this point, you will have a much clearer idea about whether you should proceed further or seek help. Then, if you choose to solicit outside help you can put it to use in ways that will benefit you most. After all, you know more about the idiosyncrasies of your company than any outsider. A series of educational events may be necessary prior to the first meeting where you begin to plan the plan. Get your transition team thinking about the challenges ahead. Educational events that might serve as primers include: seminars on quality management, reengineering, and change management. Conferences on industry trends and strategies, global competition, and domestic and international economics may also be helpful.

When you feel reasonably confident that you have the right mix of team players, you have passed a significant hurdle. You still may discover shortcomings later on in the planning process. That's alright. Course corrections are part of any planning process.

Internal Help

Once you have decided you do need help, you needn't immediately turn to a consultant to find it. Organizations of even modest size are loaded with a diverse range of talent in their employees, who possess a dazzling array of skills and knowledge. This often untapped resource can be one of your best and cheapest sources of help. Many misguided transition planners assume that individuals located further down in the organization do not offer the caliber of expertise necessary to help their more senior colleagues on the transition planning team. Yet junior employees offer a rich source of skills, knowledge, ideas, and capabilities. Turning to employees in the organization for help first serves the dual function of using talent that already exists and providing an opportunity to involve and further develop this human resource at minimal cost compared to the cost of retaining an outside consultant.

Using internal resources does not imply that your sources of help must be involved in transition planning full time. To the contrary, adding internal helpers to the team could compromise the integrity of the transition planning effort. Rather, selected individuals internal to the organization would have intermittent involvement in the planning process.

How do you locate these internal resources? Advertise down through the management ranks, requesting specific areas of expertise in benchmarking and data collection, manufacturing and service knowledge, market trends, and product development. Interview interested candidates as you would for any other job. Look closely at certain functional areas in the organization to see if there are accessible employees or pockets of employees in specialized areas.

External Help

Looking outside the organization yields a wider selection of talent and skills, but it is also trickier. I would wager a guess that most organizations select external help in a haphazard way. Many organizations are guru junkies—they become infatuated with the author of the hottest new book, the best public speaker, the consultant who helps another company they admire. This selection process does not guarantee that you will find someone aligned with your particular needs. Disappointingly, what works well in one environment will not necessarily produce the same results in another. You may find a bright, gifted individual who has something important to say. Her contribution to the field of management and organizational science may be great but she may have little to contribute to your immediate circumstance.

Beware of partial solutions to systemic problems. A transition tends to be a large, complex event in the life of an organization. Partial solutions or approaches can drive your organization off course, promoting an agenda that is based on a project or initiative and not on your organization's overall needs. I say this with a great deal of certainty. Probably one of the most difficult tasks an organization experiences in addressing transition is creating a comprehensive approach (plan) to address a comprehensive problem (transition).

To prevent the problem of partial or haphazard solutions, figure out the initial parameters, strengths, and weaknesses inherent in your team and in any planning process you conceive. Extrapolate your gaps to determine what an external expert could contribute to your effort. Hopefully, this book will help guide your thought process in this regard. After you have exhausted all internal sources to meet these needs, identify the external resources available to you. Talk with other organizations about their experiences with individual consultants or consulting firms. Ask your employees if they know of anyone or any firm that has done good work for another company. Consider running an ad in the newspaper. This action may produce hundreds of applicants, but an extensive selection process for both internal and external help is reasonable considering the importance of the task at hand. Get the best help available. The selection process itself should be a significant educational experience for the transition planning team. If it's not, you may be treating the subject too lightly.

Once you identify the top candidates to help you in your planning effort, test them with the full transition planning team. See how they respond to your initial approach. Test your assumptions. Is there any substance there? How do they respond to hypothetical questions and situations you anticipate in your planning process? Above all, be wary of your tendency to be drawn magnetically toward the all-knowing, all-seeing, I've-got-the-solution guru.

External resources are diverse and abundant. There are consulting firms that specialize in planning, and they probably should be your first order of investigation. There are also a variety of consultants and firms that specialize in a particular niche or initiative. Again, beware of "We do it all" groups or those that promote a particular initiative as a comprehensive solution in any transition. I have yet to see a single initiative that meets all the needs of a transitioning organization. That's why it is so dangerous for an organization to get caught up in implementing a single initiative, or several initiatives that are run simultaneously but independently of one another. Many organizational needs are left unaddressed. Let the transitional requirements of your organization determine the types of initiatives you employ—not vice versa.

Another word of caution: Try to avoid becoming a consultant's research and development laboratory. Most consultants are constantly evolving their techniques, skills, and knowledge. There is, of course, no better place to do this than at a client's place of business, with the client footing the bill and in an environment where there is a sense of urgency to try anything that will improve financial performance. In their fury to do something—anything—management may do whatever a consultant advises. As a result, the organization frequently becomes a testing ground for new theories and concepts. This is great for the consultant, and it can be great for the organization if it works. But chances are that the combination of risk and additional time requirements associated with trying something untested outweighs the benefits, and the organization comes out on the short end of the stick. Organizations do not have the time or resources to engage in huge amounts of experimentation during transition.

How do you prevent yourself from becoming an object of experimentation? Check references thoroughly. If a consultant cannot show you specifically how he can help you and what he intends to do, with specific examples that are relevant to your environment, move on to the next candidate. If he cannot communicate in a language that makes sense to you, with processes and models and concepts you can easily understand, look for someone else. See how well this individual can articulate an understanding of your needs. This should help tell you how aligned his approach is with your needs.

Industry affiliations and support groups are becoming an increasingly valuable source of external help. For this to provide timely value, you will need to think of it as a savings account: it will require a long-term resource investment but it will be there when you need it.

Choose your help carefully. Transitions don't start or end in a day. Even though you may be eager, or even desperate to get a plan in place—which means get help—invest the time to methodically and thoroughly consider all options.

Epilogue

Whatever the quality of a company's assets or business, in the final analysis what counts is management.

—*Sumner Redstone*

This epilogue is directed at the individual with primary responsibility for overseeing the transition plan. If that person is not the CEO, president, owner, or most senior officer or manager in the business unit that is planning for transition, you are already headed for trouble. All positions but the top are weak ones from which to leverage change. This doesn't mean that change from a middle management position is always undesirable. Sometimes the change has a localized effect—only one division or several business units are affected. In this case, it is possible that lower level managers can drive the transition effectively. From a transition management standpoint, however, it is most desirable to corral all change activity under one umbrella, from the top down. In order to do this, planning must begin at the highest appropriate level of the organization. But getting this group to sponsor and stay the course can be like herding cats. This grim reality renders many organizations simply incapable of systemic, large-scale change.

Transition strategies must be comprehensive enough, and sustained long enough, to allow for a positive impact on the organization. Large organizations tend to change slowly, not overnight. There are periods when the transition planning team and its stakeholders must keep their hands off and allow the plan to do its work. It may be reasonable to expect improvements in organizational performance six, twelve and eighteen months down the line, but not after just one month or even one quarter. It is not unusual to see a perfectly good transition planning effort get derailed when stakeholders, dissatisfied with results in the first quarter, overreact and pull the plug on the whole operation. They may try to reorganize the management team or get new leadership in place, while in actuality, all they needed to do was wait long enough for the transition plan to work. For example, a Canadian-based holding company terminated one of its subsidiary company presidents for poor financial performance. Another executive was placed in the job. Two months later, the subsidiary's performance surged, stock price followed. The new executive hadn't implemented any new initiatives, restructured, or increased market share. From a consultant's view, I believe that the transition plan developed and implemented by the original management team was on target. They were not allowed the time for the plan to work. As we discussed in Chapter 8 had the past president managed stakeholder perception more effectively, maybe this scenario could have been prevented.

If you have the responsibility for running your company (or business unit), do not relinquish authority or control for overseeing the transition planning process at any point. Your discomfort with transition is good. It will keep you on your toes. Change tends to be uncomfortable even when we want to change. Planning for transition evokes these feelings, even though nothing as of yet has changed. Stay in control. Stay involved. Be open and flexible. Be willing to step backwards and retest assumptions or plans. Be forgiving of yourself and others. All will not go as planned. Above all, devote the time necessary to create and introduce an effective transition plan.

To start a transition off on the right foot, spend the front-end time necessary to get the commitment of the most senior managers. If the transitional event is serious enough, the life of the company is probably already threatened. It may be necessary to replace some key individuals as a first step to altering traditional management approaches and increasing the speed of implementing the transition. A reasonable infusion of new perspective and experience in the senior ranks of an organization can offer many positive benefits.

Many change events occur so quickly (change in market conditions; shift in consumer spending due to economic signals) that it is crucial to respond to them quickly as well. Unfortunately, this doesn't allow for learning that may take years to achieve. For example, it can take most managers years to understand, master, and apply quality improvement in their specific organization—but the customer demands it today. Those charged with the responsibility of managing the transition must be able to assimilate new attitudes and duties very quickly. New talent may be required to get a transitional effort started on the right foot. The only alternative may be a significantly slower response to change as the organization's current leaders come up to speed. This forces people further down in the organization (who need to adapt to change and respond to new performance demands placed on them by management) to orchestrate a piecemeal approach to change from the bottom up and the middle down—because they are not dealing with change on a total organizational scale. This offers a bleak prospect for achieving an ultimately successful transition. An unempowered but dedicated group of people are stuck with a charter that has an inherently low probability of ever being accomplished. Everyone involved gets frustrated because there are too many barriers; top management is not on the transition bandwagon. Symptoms of this condition include high turnover of valued, experienced middle managers and key professionals, and a decrease in company loyalty.

Prevention is the best solution. Set your transition up for success from the start. Here are some parting thoughts:

1. Manage transition from the top of the organization or lobby for the highest appropriate level of ownership.
2. Mentally commit to adequate planning time. This may mean one month or as long as a year. Don't confuse procrastination with planning. Procrastination is what people do during transition when they don't have a clear path to follow. The planning process itself is one of discovery, education, and focus. All of which are necessary during transition.
3. Objectively estimate your ability to partake in the task at hand and add resources as necessary.
4. Outline your transition planning process. I offer you (without bias) the one presented here as an initial model to follow.
5. Assemble your planning team and have them critique and revise your outline.
6. Communicate your intentions to the organization.
7. Stay the course.

It must be remembered that there is nothing more difficult to plan, more uncertain of success, nor more dangerous to manage than the creation of a new order of things.

—Niccolo Machiavele

Bibliography

Ansoff, H.I. and Sullivan, P.A. (1991), "Strategic Responses to Environmental Turbulence," in Kilmann, R.H., Kilmann, I., and associates, *Making Organizations Competitive*, San Francisco: Jossey-Bass

Argyris, C. (1983), *Strategy, Change, and Defensive Routines*, Boston: Pitman

Argyris, C. (1986), "Skilled Incompetence," *Harvard Business Review* September/October 1986

Argyris, C. (1990), *Overcoming Organizational Defenses*, Needham Heights: Simon and Schuster

Bateson, G. (1972), *Steps to an Ecology of Mind*, New York: Ballantine

Beckhard, R. and Harris, R. (1979), *Organization Transitions: Managing Complex Change*, Reading, Mass.: Addison-Wesley

Below, P.J., Morrisey, G.L., and Acomb, B.L. (1989), *The Executive Guide to Strategic Planning*, San Francisco: Jossey-Bass

Bennis, W. (1989), *On Becoming a Leader*, Reading, Mass.: Addison-Wesley

Blake, R.R. and Mouton, J.S. (1969), *Building a Dynamic Corporation Through Grid Organization Development*, Reading Mass.: Addison-Wesley

Block, P. (1986), *The Empowered Manager*, San Francisco: Jossey-Bass

Bolman, L.G. and Deal, T.E. (1984), *Modern Approaches to Understanding and Managing Organizations*, San Francisco: Jossey-Bass

Brandt, S.C. (1986), *Entrepreneuring in Established Companies*, Homewood, Ill.: Dow-Jones Irwin

Bridges, W. (1988), *Surviving Corporate Transition*, New York: Doubleday

Burke, W.W. (1987), *Organization Development: A Normative View*, Reading Mass.: Addison-Wesley

Coch, L. and French, J.R.P. (1984), "Overcoming resistance to change," *Human Relations*, 1:512–532

Cohen, M.D., March, J.G., and Olsen, J.P. (1976), "A Garbage Can Model of Organizational Choice" *Administrative Science Quarterly*, 17:1–25

Collins, J.C. and Lazier, W.C. (1992), *Beyond Entrepreneurship*, Englewood Cliffs, N.J.: Prentice-Hall

Cyert, R.M. and March, J.G. (1963), *A Behavior Theory of the Firm* Englewood-Cliffs, N.J.: Prentice-Hall

Davis, S. and Davidson, B. (1991), *2020 Vision*, New York: Simon and Schuster

de Geus, A.P. (1988), "Planning as Learning," *Harvard Business Review* (March/April)

Deming, W.E. (1986), *Out of the Crisis* Cambridge Mass: MIT Center for Advanced Engineering Study

DePree, M. (1989), *Leadership Is an Art*, New York: Doubleday Dell Publishing Group

Egelhoff, W.G. (1993), "Great Strategy or Great Strategy Implementation–Two Ways of Competing in Global Markets," *Sloan Management Review* (Winter)

Galbraith, J.R. (1973), *Designing Complex Organizations*, Reading, Mass.: Addison-Wesley

Greiner, L.E. (1972), "Evolution and Revolution as Organizations Grow," *Harvard Business Review* (July/August)

Hampden-Turner, C. (1990), *Charting the Corporate Mind*, New York: The Free Press

Handy, C. (1989), *The Age of Unreason*, Boston: Harvard Business School Press

Hanna, D.P., (1988), *Designing Organizations for High Performance*, Reading, Mass.: Addison-Wesley

Harrison, M.I. (1987), *Diagnosing Organizations*, Newbury Park, Calif.: Sage

Herzberg, F. (1987), "One More Time: How Do You Motivate Employees?", *Harvard Business Review*, (September/October)

Hirschman, A.O. (1970), *Exit, Voice, and Loyalty: Responses to*

Decline in Firms, Organizations, and States Cambridge Mass.: Harvard University Press

Hunt, D.K. (1984), "Of Boxes, Bubbles, and Effective Management," *Harvard Business Review* (May/June)

Jacques, E. (1989) *Requisite Organization: The CEO's Guide to Creative Structure and Leadership*, Arlington, Virg.: Cason Hall

Kanter, R.M. (1984), *The Changemasters*, London: Allen and Unwin

Kanter, R.M. (1989), "The New Managerial Work," *Harvard Business Review* (November/December)

Kanter, R. M., Stein, B.A., and Jick, T.D. (1992), *The Challenge of Organizational Change*, New York: The Free Press

Kaplan, A. (1964), *The Conduct Inquiry*, San Francisco: Chandler

Kidder, J.T. (1981), *The Soul of the New Machine*, Boston: Little Brown and Company

Kilmann, R.H. (1989), *Managing Beyond the Quick Fix: A Completely Integrated Program for Creating and Maintaining Organizational Success*, San Francisco: Jossey-Bass

Kilmann, R., Kilmann, I., and associates (eds.) (1991), *Making Organizations Competitive* San Francisco: Jossey-Bass

Kotter, J.P. (1990), "What Leaders Really Do," *Harvard Business Review* (May/June)

Kotter, J.P. and Heskett, J.L. (1992), *Corporate Culture and Performance*, New York: The Free Press

Kuhn, T.S. (1970), *The Structure of Scientific Revolutions*, Chicago: University of Chicago Press (2nd edition)

Lawler, E.E. (1986), *High Involvement Management*, San Francisco: Jossey-Bass

Lawrence, P.R. and Lorsch, J.W. (1969), *Developing Organizations: Diagnosis and Action*, Reading, Mass.: Addison-Wesley

Lippitt, G., Langseth, P., and Mossop, J. (1985), *Implementing Organizational Change*, San Francisco: Jossey-Bass

Locke, E.E. (1986), "Participation in Decision Making: When Should it Be Used?" *Organizational Dynamics* (Winter)

Lynch, D. and Kordis, P.L. (1988), *Strategy of the Dolphin*, New York: Fawcett Columbine

March, J.G. (1981), "Footnotes to Organizational Change," *Administrative Science Quarterly*, 26:563–577

Michael, D.N. (1973), *On Learning to Plan and Planning to Learn* San Francisco: Jossey-Bass

Mintzberg, I. (1976), "Planning on the Left Side—Managing on the Right" *Harvard Business Review* (July/August)

Naisbitt, J. (1982), *Megatrends: Ten New Directions Transforming Our Lives*, New York: Warner Books

Odiorne, G.S. (1965), *Management by Objectives: A System of Managerial Leadership*, New York: Pitman

Ohmae, K. (1982), *The Mind of the Strategist*, New York: McGraw-Hill

Porrass, J. (1987), *Stream Analysis: A Powerful Way to Diagnose and Manage Organizational Change*, Reading, Mass.: Addison-Wesley

Rogers, E.M. (1983), *Diffusion of Innovations*, New York: The Free Press

Schein, E. (1985), *Organizational Culture and Leadership*, San Francisco: Jossey-Bass

Schein, E. (1993) "How Can Organizations Learn Faster? The Challenge of Entering the Green Room" *Sloan Management Review* (Winter)

Schein, E.H. (1969), *Process Consultation: Its Role in Organization Development*, Reading Mass.: Addison-Wesley

Schon, D.A. (1971), *Beyond the Stable State*, New York: Random House

Stata, R. (1989), "Organizational Learning: The Key to Management Innovation," *Sloan Management Review*, No. 63, Spring

Thompson, J.D. (1967), *Organizations in Action*, New York: McGraw-Hill

Tichy, N.M. (1983), *Managing Strategic Change*, New York: John Wiley and Sons

van der Rohe, M. (1991), "Thoughts on the Business of Life" *Forbes* Aug. 19, 1991, p. 152

Wack, P. (1985), "Scenarios: Uncharted Waters Ahead," *Harvard Business Review* (September/October)

Watzlawick, P., Beavin, J.H., and Jackson, D. (1967), *Pragmatics of Human Communication*, New York: W.W. Norton

Weisbord, M. (1987), *Productive Workplaces: Organizing and Managing for Dignity, Meaning, and Community*, San Francisco: Jossey-Bass

Zemke, R. and Schaf, R. (1989), *The Service Edge: 101 Companies That Profit from Customer Service*, Markham, Ontario: Penguin Books

Index